words

words

Reflections on the uses of language

British Broadcasting Corporation

Published by the
British Broadcasting Corporation
35 Marylebone High Street
London W1M 4AA

ISBN: 0 563 12768 6
First Published 1975
Reprinted 1976

Printed in Great Britain by
Tonbridge Printers Ltd
Peach Hall Works
Shipbourne Road
Tonbridge Kent

Contents

Preface

'Words', wrote Thomas Hobbes in 1651, 'are wise men's counters, they do but reckon with them, but they are the money of fools'; a definition which gets the contributors to this book with both barrels, because in different ways we are all professionally concerned with the use of words in earning our living.

Words are to radio what pictures are to television – the basic raw material. They describe situations and express thoughts, they stir our emotions and touch our imagination. The essays in this book are essentially reflections on the uses of language. They were written as talks for the Radio 3 series 'Words' in 1973 and 1974 and they are printed here substantially as they were broadcast.

Robert Louis Stevenson, writing more than 200 years after the author of Leviathan, took a rather more romantic view of language:

'Bright is the ring of words
When the right man rings them'.

Broadcast words, of course, are never rung just by those who write them and speak them at the microphone. These talks were produced by Robert Fox and Anthony Rendell, and the austere Broadcasting House tradition of anonymity which masked their identity does not diminish their contribution.

The largest debt to be recorded, however, is to George Fischer, a man relentlessly and unfashionably concerned with the importance of the English language. The idea for the series was his, and he simply went on about it until he got it on the air.

Ian McIntyre

Ian McIntyre

Words

The only two things I know about Herbert Spencer are that Carlyle called him 'the most immeasurable ass in Christendom', which wasn't very nice, and that someone once told him that to play billiards well was the sign of an illspent youth. I came across some signs of my own illspent youth the other day in the shape of some old Order Papers from the Union at Cambridge. Order Papers of debates for which I'd selected the motions.

'That the middle-classes are morally corrupt'. That's got a fine ringing tone to it. I wonder what it actually meant? 'That too many people talk too much'. Yes, well that still makes quite a lot of sense today. 'That this House dislikes definitions'. That one puzzles me. Disraeli made somebody say something like it in *Vivian Gray*, I think, and it may have been a precious echo of the master. But if it was the aberration was temporary. A few years later, as a very new BBC producer, I remember coming under fire from a formidable lady colleague at a Third Programme meeting for suggesting a talk about dictionaries. She seemed to find the proposal either Teutonic or frivolous or in some curious way both Teutonic and frivolous at the same time and could only register incredulity. 'Do you read Bradshaw in your spare time, too?' she enquired. Native stubbornness thrust me firmly into the arms of jesting Pilate. 'Of course,' I said, 'frequently. Don't you?'

Two questions I've never come to any very firm conclusions about are what sort of people make the best dictionary-makers and how the best dictionaries are made. Recently in

Paris I met Paul Robert, the man who has done more for the reputation of French lexicography than any man since Littré. Though with the Dictionary of the French Academy still nibbling pedantically away at the very beginning of the alphabet, I suppose it could be argued that he hadn't much to compete with. Anyway, a less probable background for a lexicographer than Paul Robert would be difficult to imagine. He came from a family settled, since the middle of the nineteenth century, in Algeria. In 1939 he was studying law. After wartime experience of cyphers he resumed his studies and wrote a thesis on citrus fruits. The dictionary began almost as a hobby – a modest and purely private undertaking to fashion a tool for his own use.

An eighteenth-century compatriot of his, Antoine de Rivereau, said that working on his dictionary reminded him of an amorous doctor who found himself obliged to dissect the body of his mistress. Robert was much more in the position of a complete layman setting out to write a rival to Gray's Anatomy, and he succeeded brilliantly.

As a guide to literary taste and to temperament I don't suppose a liking for definitions indicates anything more alarming than a preference for the orderly over the confused, or for the classical over the romantic.

Some men of letters, of course, have taken the view that the making of definitions is altogether too serious a matter to be left to the lexicographers. Flaubert's *Dictionary of Received Ideas* comes to mind, with its definition of tarmacadam as 'a substance which put an end to revolution by doing away with the means of making street barricades'.

In America someone who produced a notable line in definitions was Ambrose Bierce. A saint – 'A dead sinner, revised and edited'. Meekness – 'Uncommon patience in planning a revenge that is worthwhile'. Best of all perhaps his definition of a hand, which managed to combine the sardonic with the surrealist. The hand – 'A singular instrument, worn at the end of the human arm, and commonly thrust into somebody's pocket'.

A man, I'd have thought, who played a pretty dangerous game of billiards.

A French widow in every bedroom

I wouldn't want to give the impression that in the matter of language my position is analogous to those who oppose the addition of fluoride to our drinking water. On the other hand I do experience a spasm of irritation when the newspapers go suddenly and rather mindlessly overboard for a not particularly elegant usage like 'mugging'.

If the word itself isn't of more than passing interest, the way it was received here is revealing. There was, inevitably, a flurry of correspondence in *The Times*. Mr Robert Carr solemnly favoured the House of Commons with a definition of the word which was pedestrian even by Home Office standards; best of all, one morning in November at the Old Bailey, Judge Cussen struck a notable blow for the English language by reproving counsel for using the word in addressing the court. 'The resources of the English language are not so meagre,' he observed tartly, 'as to require yet another transatlantic importation'.

I'm not sure that the judge is right, as a matter of fact. I suspect that once the lexicographers have given it a proper doing over, mugging may well turn out to be a bit of old English thieves' cant making a return journey across the Atlantic. Still, I don't find it altogether easy to dismiss the sneaking suspicion that we are living on linguistic capital in this country, and to the assertion that the great majority of us no longer make positive creative use of the language, I wouldn't feel able to dredge up more than one qualification. Elaine Morgan, in her book *The Descent of Women*, said that Wordsworth had got it all wrong about children when he spoke about them trailing clouds of glory. This isn't the place to argue the point theologically, but linguistically, any parent of small children knows she is wrong. My six-year-old daughter stood watching my wife signing a cheque the other day and then announced that her writing was better than mine. 'Oh, really?' said my wife, 'Yes,' said Katharine firmly, 'Daddy's writing doesn't hang together'. And then, just in case my wife hadn't grasped the distinction, she added, 'It's flickety'.

Well, I must clearly write a letter, in my best flickety hand, to Dr George Steiner, because in the *New York Times* the other month he was expressing much more than a sneaking suspicion about linguistic flabbiness. 'The centre of linguistic gravity,' he wrote, 'the energy core, has passed away from England. It's no longer in the British Isles that the English language is being spoken and written at the highest levels of inventive intensity'.

One can accept Dr Steiner's general point without agreeing with him that the author of *Portnoy's Complaint* has reached that highest level of inventive intensity. And so long as we stop short of fabricating myths. I don't believe there ever was a time when we all wrote and spoke like angels.

And if we're fussed about being relegated to the second division, there are numbers of things we could do about it. We could, for instance, be less dismissive about out-of-London speech forms, because surely it is in our regional dialects and in Wales and Scotland that much of the vigour of the English language lies. It's been said for years now that radio and television are killing them. Did anyone who thinks so see or hear the interviews with a Suffolk man who unearthed a twelfth-century figure while hoeing sugar beet? It just isn't true. What is nearer the truth, perhaps, is that dialect is still painfully widely regarded as a language that hasn't quite made it; 'Dialect words,' said Thomas Hardy, 'those terrible marks of the beast to the truly genteel'.

Gentility has a lot to answer for, and there's still far too much of it in the way that English is taught to some of our children – an almost manic concern with rooting out grammatical error to the exclusion of all else. If grammar were everything, after all, there would be nothing to find fault with in Hoffnung's celebrated Tyrolean hotel brochure – 'A French widow in every bedroom affording delightful prospects'.

A modest plea, therefore – to those who teach and those who examine, to those who write the textbooks and those who publish them – a plea simply that they should take a more generative view of what it's all about. That might afford even more delightful prospects than a French widow in every bedroom – and it would certainly be very good for Judge Cussen's blood pressure.

The case of the fornicating shovel

Whenever I see a snow scene by Breughel I think of Catterick Camp and the winter of 1955, a period I spent being trained as a trooper in the Armoured Corps. One of my companions in misery was a boy from Wiltshire, who was heavily fixated on the four-letter word that was subsequently to prove such a money-spinner for Mr Kenneth Tynan. My fellow-trooper's name was Whitehouse, oddly enough, and one day I suggested to him that in the interest of greater precision he ought occasionally to use the word fornicate instead. Irony alas, is a treacherous device. Trooper Whitehouse never called a spade a spade in my hearing again – always a fornicating shovel.

He came to my mind when his equally fixated namesake was complaining to the BBC about Chuck Berry's song 'My ding-a-ling'. The frontiers of what is taboo in language and speech are constantly shifting; anyone who thinks that you have to travel to Polynesia to find a taboo in good working order these days is mistaken. Indeed the student of taboos in language could do worse than start in contemporary America and work his way backwards.

One dictionary, published in the United States, has a self-congratulatory preface in which it announces that its pages are unsullied by any words smacking of intolerance between the races. Anyone who wants to know what Agatha Christie meant when she wrote a book called *Ten Little Niggers* will have to shop around for a work of reference by someone still degenerate enough to believe that there is a connection between dictionary making and scientific method.

Edward Gibbon, who lived at a time when the word taboo was only just finding its way into the English language, devised a characteristically sly way of eating his cake and having it. 'My English text is chaste,' he wrote in his autobiography. 'All licentious passages are left in the decent obscurity of a learned language'.

The case of his contemporary Sam Johnson is rather more complex. I'd never thought of him as one to mince words particularly, but it was only when I read a new book on Johnson by the American scholar Paul Fussell that I realised the extent to which Boswell doctored his language for purposes of presentation. Generations of undergraduates have worked into their carefully rehearsed spontaneities in the Union what Johnson said to Garrick about going to visit him backstage. 'I'll come no more behind your scenes, David, for the silk stockings and white bosoms of your actresses excite my amorous propensities'. Professor Fussell points out that this is what he calls 'a version done into Johnsonese'. What was actually said was a shade less Augustan – 'No David, I will never come back. For the white bubbies and the silk stockings of your actresses excite my genitals'.

Some of the doctor's admirers may find this a distressingly coarse disclosure. Those who do may care to consider whether without his readiness to call a spade a spade we should today be continuing beneficiaries of that great work which is his dictionary.

The commonly held view of Johnson as authoritarian in matters of language is a mistaken one. The man who really wanted to invest the dictionary with an elevated and prescriptive function was Johnson's patron in the project – Lord Chesterfield. The American critic, Scott Elledge, put the matter admirably in his study *The Naked Science of Language*. 'From the beginning,' he wrote, 'Johnson's desire to explore was at odds with Chesterfield's desire to civilise'. His patron's view was that the dictionary should have an effect on the language; Johnson held that 'the laws of the life of a language are stronger than any human lawmaker'. And of course he was right. Johnson knew that usage was king and that academies of language were a nonsense; 'what is so much in the power of men as language,' he says at one point in the Plan, 'will very often be capriciously conducted'.

It was characteristic that Johnson should so readily admit to a measure of caprice himself. Thomas Hobbes got very short shrift. 'I scorned, Sir, to quote him at all,' he told Boswell, 'because I did not like his principles.'

Principles were one thing, but language was quite another. It's not certain that Johnson would have known the word nigger – the OED can't find an example of it earlier than two years after his death. He did have a view about our transatlantic cousins, though – 'I'm willing to love all mankind except an American,' he once said. If he'd known that one day they would be capable of confusing the aims of the civil rights movement with the purposes of lexicography I imagine he might have expressed himself in words that broke a number of quite different taboos simultaneously.

Gift of tongues

'I have come to the conclusion that the ritual parts of the Book of Common Prayer should be conducted not in English but in Latin. The rite, as distinct from the Ministry of the

Word, is the link between the dead and the unborn. As such, it requires a timeless language which, in practice, means a dead language'. Well now, who, in these flat, latter days can write impossible, reactionary good sense of that sort? W. H. Auden, no less. Where? In the pages of an impossible and reactionary weekly called the *New Statesman*.

Mr Auden was cheating a bit, in fact, because he was supposed to be reviewing a book called *English Biblical Translation* by A. C. Partridge, but he gives his hobby-horse the shortest of canters and has it back in its stable in no time at all.

Professor Partridge gives a sort of critical barium meal to the biblical translation of a millennium, from the Anglo-Saxon gloss above the text of the Lindisfarne Gospels to the New English Bible. His book is full of good things. Who called St Jerome the Christian Cicero? How many books of the Bible did Shakespeare quote from? Who said of the editors of the King James Bible that they had put the errors in the text and the correct reading in the margin? Who called the Book of Common Prayer an almsbasket of Papist prayers?

Professor Partridge tells us all this and a good deal more besides almost in passing, and without ever distracting attention from his major themes.

If he has a hero, it is Tyndale. It was, he said, his conviction, that 'the Hebrew tongue agreeth a thousand times more with the English than with the Latin', and one thing that emerges very clearly from this book is how much of our supposed debt to the translators of the King James Bible is in fact a debt to Tyndale. 'In him we live, move and have our being'; 'the day-spring from on high hath visited us'; 'blessed are the peacemakers'. Very often, when we salute the felicities of the Authorised Version we are in effect paying tribute to the ill-favoured youth who according to his own testimony turned to the spiritual life as a refuge from what he called 'the rage of worldly business'.

The late nineteenth and twentieth centuries have come to rival the sixteenth as an era of great Biblical activity. Partridge points out what an extraordinarily perverse talent

Bible translators have evolved for making life difficult for themselves, and cites what he sees as the mistaken directive, in commissioning the Revised Version, to limit the language of the new text to the vocabulary of Tudor and Jacobean authors. The work was faithfully carried out, certainly, but it was an anachronism – a literary equivalent of the rash of neo-Gothic churches which was also owed to the Victorians.

The brief given to those who worked on the New English Bible was to prove a bit of an albatross, too; the ideal of 'timeless' English (a phrase that seems to have been borrowed from Ronald Knox) was misconceived, and it is difficult now to dissent from the judgement of Henry Gifford: 'the translators, turning to the current speech of our own time – more stagnant than current – have shut themselves in a one-generation culture'. It rather looks as if the Jerusalem Bible, better served by its literary advisors, and with its invaluable explanations and footnotes, will prove the more durable work of the two.

The rest is silence

'He has occasional flashes of silence,' said Sidney Smith, 'that make his conversation perfectly delightful'. Well, I'm sure that Macaulay did bang on a bit – he *was* a nineteenth-century Liberal, after all – but as is so often the case with Sidney Smith, there is an oblique statement of a point of substance behind the glancing malice. Those exponents of revolutionary linguistic theory who assert that speech is not just a means of communication but a physical action ought to expand their definition, it seems to me, to accommodate silence, too.

In 1972, the Edinburgh Festival brought over the Japanese Noh Theatre. Advance booking was heavy, and there were long queues each night for the gallery. The evening I was there, there was a generous sprinkling of Italians in the audience. Most of them must have come in the same bus tour, I think, because although they were widely scattered, the time before the curtain rose was given over to a lot of long-range conversation and semaphoring to distant friends. Most of them sat down after the curtain went up, but not all stopped talking. Indeed the chattering now had added to it a good deal of cackling, occasioned by what was going on – or not going on – on the stage.

This display of Italian opera-house manners wasn't at all well received in the Athens of the North, and there was a good deal of muttering and glaring. Finally, after about 20 minutes, the Italians rose like a flock of starlings and left as noisily as they had come; the gallery was now free to give the psychological subtleties of the Tokugawa period its undivided and silent attention.

Now it's true that the miawling dialogue of the Japanese classical theatre falls very oddly on the western ear, but I think that what really got the Italians was the silence. Noh drama has an elaborate convention of what is spoken and what isn't, because a play is an imitation of coming to awareness and in this process some moments require speech for their realisation and some do not.

This all floated into my mind when I was reading a book called *Speaking and Language* – the last work of the American writer and critic Paul Goodman. 'Silence,' he writes, 'gives information, sometimes crushingly,' and he then calls the roll for a dozen different brands of the precious substance – the dumb silence of apathy; the fertile silence of awareness; the musical silence that accompanies absorbed activity; the noisy silence of resentment or self-recrimination. He has some acute things to say about one of the opposites of silence, too – what he calls the pathology of living too much in the world of speech; a world whose excessive freedom and empty verbalism derange all sense of reality and allow ideas and sentences to crowd out experience. Some doctors think this is what General Amin is suffering from, I understand. Nearer home, the uninstructed visitor to El Vino's in Fleet Street or to the BBC Club might think there had been an outbreak of it in London, but that would of course be an illusion.

Paul Goodman also deals crisply with those he describes as the champions of multi-media – those who attack literature on the ground that it is 'linear'. 'Their technique,' he says, 'is one of surrounding and engulfing people with artificial impressions. In such a process, words are trivialised or forced out, for the hearer of words must have a psychological space to interpret and respond to them in'.

Reflecting on those words, I wonder whether I wasn't a little hard earlier on those Italian visitors to the Edinburgh Festival. Perhaps they were simply reacting against the lack of psychological space in the gallery of the Lyceum Theatre. And I certainly wouldn't want to give the impression that everybody in Edinburgh has a Trappist awareness of the creative beauty of silence. I once heard Lord Boothby tell a story of being taken as a child to see the farewell appearance in the Scottish capital of some renowned ballerina of the day. At the end of the evening, the great lady sank to the boards in a last curtsey. Before the applause, there was a moment of rapt silence – broken by the voice of someone who said to her neighbour, 'She's awfully like Mrs Wishart'.

The rest, I suppose one might say, is silence.

Time to bury old John Witherspoon

Given half a chance, Scotsmen have always gone on a bit about the English language – not just English-English, but American-English, too. It was, indeed, a North-Briton who claimed to have coined the word Americanism. His name was John Witherspoon, a Church of Scotland minister who went out to be President of Princeton in 1769. When Princeton was closed by the war he went into politics, and his signature is to be found on both the Declaration of Independence and the Articles of Confederation.

His attachment to the revolution, however, did not extend to the language spoken by the revolting colonists, and two hundred years or so before Radio 3 started a series called 'Words' he was already sounding off in the pages of a Philadelphia newspaper. 'I have heard in this country,' he wrote, 'in the senate, at the bar, and from the pulpit, errors in grammar, improprieties and vulgarisms which hardly any person of the same class would have fallen into in Great Britain'. Well, I offer the quotation to Mr Nixon. He may find a use for it when he gets to the chapter in his memoirs describing his contribution to the Republican tradition.

When that tradition was still very young, many Americans saw in British attitudes to the way they spoke the language a strong element of what would today be called cultural colonialism. Travel today in Africa or Asia and you get a fair idea of what nineteenth-century Americans must have felt about the patronising tone of the self-appointed guardians of the English language. British harping on their linguistic inferiority got in the way of America's search for a national identity; it was particularly obtuse of people in this country not to appreciate how strong – and how touching – a desire there was to go on, in spite of everything, participating in the English past.

What few attempts there were at bridge-building came mainly from the American side. Noah Webster, some years before the appearance of his first dictionary, proposed a sort of joint standing committee of American and English scholars 'to consider', as he put it, 'such points of difference in the practice of the two countries as it is desirable to adjust'. The scheme foundered on the rocks of English academic hostility – not altogether surprisingly, perhaps, given Webster's rather quaint notion that the right man to direct the project on this side of the Atlantic was the Professor of Arabic at Cambridge.

For most of the nineteenth century, Americans had to put up with a good deal of ignorant nonsense from this side of the ocean. 'The Americans,' said the *Edinburgh Review*, 'make it a point of conscience to have no aristocratic distinctions – even in their vocabulary'. A slightly bizarre judgement, one might think, from that Whiggish quarter.

And America was slow to counter-attack; didn't, indeed, do so in any very determined or coherent way until well into this century, and by then it wasn't really necessary. American economic ascendancy was established, the film industry had done its work and the mutual interest the two nations took in each other, friendly or otherwise, had become far less compulsive.

The bearer of one of the sharpest lances on the American side was H. L. Mencken. When his work on the American language first appeared in 1919 some said he was animated by anti-British and pro-German sentiments during the first world war. Even if it had been true, it would have invalidated only a little of his analysis of the genius and strength of the American language. 'Confronted by novelty,' he wrote, 'the Americans always manage to fetch up a name for it that not only describes it but also illuminates it, whereas the English, since the Elizabethan stimulant oozed out of them, have been content merely to catalogue it'. Fair-minded Britons might concede that there's still a lot of truth in that today, just as fair-minded Americans would probably admit that we are less addicted than they to grinding and unlovely verbalising.

There are zealots and old-believers still on both sides of the Atlantic, but I would guess that most people today don't very much care. Of those that do, an increasing number recognises that language is not something that can be directed or controlled or nationalised or possessed in any way.

When the King on Asteroid 325 saw St Exupéry's little prince approaching he exclaimed, 'Ah, here is a subject!' And the little prince asked himself, 'How could he recognise me when he has never seen me before?' It's a good question in any language. Perhaps it would be a generous contribution to the bicentenary celebrations which loom in 1976 if we were to recognise definitively that when it is posed in the American language, there isn't really a very good answer to it in English.

Two hundred years of linguistic civil war is long enough. High time, if the ghost of old John Witherspoon will forgive the expression, to bury the hatchet.

Marghanita Laski

Unknown to Jane Austen

On panel programmes I'm often advertised as having a special interest in words, which I do. So listeners tend to send me questions about words, and the gist of many of them is to ask me to agree on how ugly the new words are.

I find this hard to understand. People aren't saying that what they find ugly is what the words stand for. It's some words themselves they dislike: words they think of as being new.

Now the oddity of this is that – science apart – there are very few new words in English. One of the great beauties and excitements of this language is its capacity for constantly giving new life to old words: by, say, adding suffixes, usually old suffixes, like -worthy and -wise; by turning nouns into verbs and vice versa; by adding prepositions to old words; and simply by changing the very meaning of words we've known for centuries. And a pleasant ploy to make this point is to invent sentences that would have been incomprehensible to Jane Austen though every word in them would have been known to her. To take a simple example: 'After so many Manhattans, better not take hash. But she needed a new face, so she propped up the baby grand and reached for her compact.' And I had to use Manhattan rather than cocktail because Jane Austen might well have heard cocktail used in our modern sense.

But you don't need to make up such sentences. You run in to them every day of the week. Take this one, from a recent American thriller: 'The short dog was rolling around on the sidewalk, spilling sweet lucy.' Here, like Jane Austen, though I know all the words, I'm not sure what they mean. I think, from the context, that a short dog is a bottle and sweet lucy is wine. But notice, there's no word there you could fairly call ugly.

You may say, that's an American example, and so not fair. All right, here's an English one, compressed from an article in *Country Life*, and what could be more English than that?

'The two doors have opening quarterlights. Front seats have ample adjustment for reach and rake. Front and rear bumpers have rubber inserts and overriders. The gearchange is springloaded to the upper ratios. On winding roads, the suspension shows up well with little roll.'

No ugly words there. No words that would have been unknown to Jane Austen in a passage that would have been incomprehensible to her. But a passage that demonstrates another ingrained habit of English which might, you'd think, have endeared new usages to people, the habit of calling new things by old names. In England at least, elevators soon became lifts, automobiles motors, locomotives engines, helicopters choppers.

Mind you, I'm not saying there aren't any new words. There are, for instance, new scientific words to an extent that takes up a third of the space in the Oxford English Dictionary's new Supplement. But these scientific words, which mostly have to be created according to strict rules, aren't, I think, the new words people object to. Few of them come into common use, and, when they do, they tend to get simplified and anglicised, as benzedrine, used as a nasty drug, takes on the endearing name of benny to go with such other pretty drug names as rainbows and red devils.

Then there are the so-called aliens, the words that come to us from abroad, and usually represent cultural enrichment. I doubt Jane Austen would have heard of the Japanese tempura or the Scandinavian smörgasbord, though she could have done. But Milton would have known Bologna sausage, Shakespeare would have known Parmesan cheese, and Chaucer probably knew ravioli.

I grant there's a certain initial difficulty in dealing with all the new *ways* an old word can deploy itself: all the new meanings a verb like 'to do,' for instance, can take on – to arrest, to copulate with, to clean your room, to say nothing of new uses of 'do up' and 'do down' and 'do with' and 'do over'. But nothing to dislike here, surely?

I rather think that the expressed dislike to new words boils down to two main things. First, specifically, new words made with -ise and -isation – finalise, capitalisation – though goodness knows why, since these suffixes are almost as old as English – who objects to civilisation? And then, deeply felt and barely comprehended a terror of new usages because they imply new ways of thinking that we are all growing too old to take in.

Thing this name

If you look up the words 'doll's house' in the *Oxford English Dictionary*'s first Supplementary volume, you will see that the earliest example of doll's house is dated 1783. Now it is perfectly likely that someone more interested in doll's houses than in dictionaries might protest that 1783 as an earliest found date was nonsense. Why, he might say, I myself have seen a doll's house of George I's day.

And so he may well have done. But the dictionary isn't interested in things. It's interested in the words that name them, and we could reasonably challenge our objector to produce evidence that the George I thing he saw was at that time called a doll's house. So far as we know, that thing was then called a baby-house. And if you look up doll's house, you won't be led to baby-house, because the *Oxford English Dic-*

tionary isn't a dictionary of concept or an encyclopedia. It is a dictionary of words, and information about the things words stand for is largely incidental.

But the point is one that often escapes the non-lexicographer as well it may. I remember an engineer who wrote to say that he had himself seen a Bailey Bridge before 1944, the dictionary's first date, and so he may have done. But was the thing he saw then called a Bailey Bridge? He probably thinks now that it was, because a tendency we all have is to back-project names on to things we knew before they got their current name. 'I well remember,' an old man might say, 'my first trip to Llandudno just before the first world war and my mother saying "If you're sick in the coach, I'll put you over my knee".' And no doubt he does remember it, and in all sincerity. But what his mother almost certainly said was not coach but charabanc.

In the fourth century St John Chrysostom said that it was not names that gave confidence in things, but things that gave confidence in names. And I often recall him when I think of manufacturers and advertisers racking their brains for fetching names for things, confident that if they can only find the right name, the thing will take. And sometimes a manufacturer's name does really take, in a big way – and then he's apt to get more than he's bargained for. Manufacturers loathe it when, for instance, instead of saying 'I'm going to vacuum the bedroom', we say, 'I'm going to hoover the bedroom', or when the manufacturer's name simply becomes figurative, as in 'She led a Rolls-Royce existence.' Because when that kind of thing happens, the relevant manufacturers picture us going into showrooms and saying, 'I want to buy a hoover – or a rolls-royce' – with a small h or two small r's – and the salesman replying, 'Yes, madam – or sir – and what make of hoover or rolls-royce do you want?' For manufacturers want their names to name only *their* things. These names have lost all value for them when they name everybody else's things of the same kind as well.

There seems to be no rhyme nor reason in names, why one takes and not another, or why, having taken, a name should vanish and be replaced. In the 1890s, when people took snapshots, they would say they were kodaking. Kodak films go on, the name kodaking doesn't. No group of people looks more frenetically for new names than the world of fashion, yet periodically – at least from 1599 and possibly from 1390 – a garment has come into fashion whose only right name, for the time being, seems to be sack. The volume of the dictionary in which this appears went to press before the first world war, and the then editors surmised that this use of sack had become obsolete. But we, who lived through the 1960s know that it hadn't.

So when we readers for the dictionary need examples of names, the things they name are absolutely useless to us. We can be surrounded by, say, Charollais cattle and jelly-babies and hoovers; we can have the clearest memories of cat's whiskers and rumbas in nightclubs and the introduction of synchromesh gears; we can go to museums and stare at piecrust tables and Ming china and Battersea boxes. As dictionary readers the only evidence for us these things exist is when someone has written down their names in a dated text. And there is no present evidence for us that the things called Battersea boxes existed in the eighteenth century when the things we now call Battersea boxes were made.

On not saying the unspeakable

If you ask people to say aloud, 'I wish that the person I most love will die in pain after a lingering disease,' hardly anyone will. Intellectuals say, why should they, when it isn't true. Non-intellectuals say, more honestly, that they somehow don't feel they'd like to.

Our feelings that words said aloud, made flesh, have real and magical power seems to be as potent as ever it was. We all know of past examples – of the Chinese who are said not to have named their children till they were sure they would survive, of the Romans, who according to De Quincy, concealed the name of their city lest their enemies conjured with it, and of the magic of Abracadabra and 'Open Sesame'. And today there are still people who believe they can call the devil by saying Mass backwards, to say nothing of those who address their gods by more formal prayers. Even today the Jews don't speak the name of their god aloud and have in their prayerbook a form of change of name for someone dangerously ill – presumably to deceive the Angel of Death. And even today the words we use *about* our language still carry so much magical significance as to suggest that once a person who could speak had so much power he must be a magician. We spell words and we use the same word for casting spells, changing the very course of nature. Our word *grammar* once meant magic – the older form *grammarye* still has this meaning. We use the French form *grimoire* for a black-magic book, and our modern glamour, another form of grammar, still has traces of the magical meaning.

Our beliefs that words have magical connotations often lead us into great silliness, especially since we seldom recognise what it is we're doing. One of the most common methods of social reform in this country is reform by nomenclature – we leave things as they are, but change what we call them. Thus the dole becomes a social benefit and the poor become the disadvantaged and terminal asylums become sunset homes. And anything to do with class had become unsayable to such an extent that we're no longer capable of examining the phenomenon.

But our oddest behaviour is with the so-called dirty words, which include all the proper names for anything bodily we don't like to talk about. It's well known that we've never had a non-euphemistic English name for what the upper classes are currently calling the lavatory and the lower classes the toilet, and even these names are too bold for some people who go along the passage or ask if you know the geography. But the strangest of all is our treatment of such words as those till recently written as f – dash and c – dash.

I'm sure that when you heard me say f – dash and c – dash you heard in your minds the words these euphemisms stand for. I'm certain that these words form in your mind when you see the equivocations on the printed page. But many of you are still appalled to see the words printed in full and if I said them on the radio, many of you would erupt in letters of protest. But I shall be very much surprised if you are offended enough to write angrily at what I've said so far – even though, as a result, these words have undoubtedly passed through your minds. The offence arises when they actually exist, in print or in sound, in full.

I must confess that I don't understand this at all, and maybe it isn't understandable. Maybe we need a range of words to be offended by, as we seem to need currently barely permissible swearwords which have to be shocking to be effective. But where does the magic lie that can cause such terror or affront? It's not in the intention, or people wouldn't, I hope, be afraid to say that they wished their loved ones would die in pain. And it's certainly not in any inherent quality of the words, unrelated to meaning, as I hope to prove to you, by confronting you with two words I found in facing pages of the *Oxford English Dictionary*'s new Supplement. Both were unknown to me, and I am reasonably confident that both will be unknown to almost all of you. One of them is obscene – or, rather, names an act that many people would consider obscene. If there is any inherent nastiness in these unknown words, one of them will shock you, the other leave you cold. The two words, in alphabetical order, are gamahuche and gametangium. Well, did either of these hurt – as it would have hurt if I'd said f – dash or c – dash in full?

Deep deep feeling

There's a story by O. Henry called *Proof of the Pudding* in which an editor and a journalist argue about the language people are likely to use when under great stress. The editor maintains that in such a situation a man or woman would speak in elevated tones, the journalist that they'd use the simplest everyday speech. Still arguing they go to the journalist's home and discover a note to say that their two wives have run away to make their livings on the stage. At which the journalist, who had pressed the claims of everyday speech, cries out 'My God, why hast thou given me this cup to drink!', while the editor blurts out, 'Say, shack, ain't that a hell of a note?'

Well, whatever people may do spontaneously in such situations, there is no doubt that our considered convention is for the utmost formality. Colloquial speech is for a gamut of situations ranging from ordinary everyday life to stage comedy. The serious events of life demand the most formal speech we can manage.

When I'm reading books for the *Oxford English Dictionary*, looking for early examples of words and phrases, I know that when my writer gets solemn I'm going to find nothing, because when he gets solemn his language gets formal, which is to say, old-fashioned, totally lacking any of the novelties or colloquialisms of his time. Take, as an example, Jane Austen – it's often useful to take Jane Austen. She is one of the liveliest letter-writers in English. She wrote her letters almost as she must have spoken, and these letters have been one of the OED's richest sources of early colloquial usage in her time. Of her brother's London house, she writes, 'It is a delightful place, and the garden is quite a love', and, of a possible second edition of *Mansfield Park*, 'Though I like praise as well as anybody, I like what Edward calls "Pewter" too'. But when her father dies in 1805, she writes to her brother at sea, 'Our dear Father has closed his virtuous and happy life. Heavy as is the blow, we can already feel that a thousand comforts remain to us to soften it. Next to that of the consciousness of his worth and constant preparation for another world, is the remembrance of his having suffered, comparatively speaking, nothing.'

There is nothing here to suggest it is Jane Austen writing. When death strikes closely, she instinctively adopts the formal style that seems inseparable from that solemn event –

but why does it? Why would it be unthinkable to write a letter of condolence that began, 'I'm awfully sorry to get the whisper that your old man's kicked the bucket'? Why is the sincerity of informal speech inappropriate for an occasion when one might have thought sincerity entirely in place? Yet, for death, even the most formal English has sometimes not seemed formal enough. There was a time when important epitaphs were always written in Latin.

The late Gilbert Harding once observed that the best manners in marriage are to be seen in the icy politeness that accompanies a marital row. 'If it isn't too much trouble, would you be so kind as to pass me the newspaper?' instead of 'Throw over the paper.' Maybe the best way to make up quarrels would be to revert to normal speech again. But for some occasions normal speech is unthinkable. It would be unthinkable to crown the monarch, for instance, in modern colloquial English, and we all know the endless discussions as to whether church services should be in Latin or in English, in the old formal English or in something more up to date. The present tendency seems to be for modernisation, but I think it's probably wrong, in view of the intended ends. People don't so much want to understand religion as to feel it deeply, and the desire for formal language on solemn occasions seems common to all classes. Even that most dreadful of all formal languages, politicians' English, is probably what's expected of the creatures, and if politicians spoke naturally and spontaneously, their audiences might well feel they hadn't been approached with respect.

But for me at least, except in the words and voice of a master, formal language is never effective. And in the real-life tragedies of people who can't manage the formal language at all, there is nothing so moving as the broken ordinary speech that doesn't even try to be grand.

A stroll down Wardour Street

Since a large part of dictionary work consists of looking for unrecorded words or earlier examples of recorded words, you might reasonably assume that to look for such words in historical novels would be fruitless. Historical novels seek to recreate the past, and, being later than that past, can hardly antedate it. But in fact historical novels can be as useful as any other reading, some of the reasons for this being reputable, others less so.

Let's take some of the reputable ones first. An historical novelist, who has examined the material of his chosen period, may revive some words which have passed out of use before his time but which, as a result of his use of them, come back into the language, at least as archaisms. Thus Sir Walter Scott revived *gramarye*, which is still in archaic use – Kipling spoke of England as 'Merlin's isle of gramarye'.

Then an historical novelist who uses a foreign setting may introduce foreign words and phrases, not known in England in the period he is writing about, but which have become common here since. In a novel with a late-medieval Swiss setting, *Anne of Geierstein*, Scott uses the word *minnesinger*, a word now known to everyone interested in medieval European lays. But the word wasn't known in medieval English when the minnesingers were current.

A more dubious practice by historical novelists is their use of names or nicknames that have come into being later than the event or person they commemorate. There is no evidence that Queen Mary I of England was known as Bloody Mary in her own day, and if an historical novelist made Mary's contemporaries refer to her as Bloody Mary, he could show no justification for it. But since Bloody Mary is a phrase that now exists and is properly recorded in the dictionary, historical novelists can provide as good evidence for the existence of this phrase as anyone else can.

And this brings us to the question: how far *are* historical novelists justified in using language that didn't exist at the time they are writing about? Obviously, to create suspension of disbelief, they must take *some* care. There was no credibility in a novel I read, set some seventy years ago, in which a young girl spoke of a 'three-piece band' at a ball. Older historical novelists often sought credibility by using the fustian language that used to be called Wardour Street English, peppering their pages with such phrases as 'By my halidom' and 'Grammercy of your courtoisie, gentle knight.' This we have discarded, to fall, I believe, into an opposite error and especially in children's historical stories, that of using a modern or nearly modern language in order to show that the people of the past were really just like us.

But, of course, they weren't. We are what we can say, and people who can't use the languages of, say, politics of the left or *angst* are unlike us in important ways. But to confine ourselves to the languages of the past would be a pointless exercise. Even though we used no words not existing in the earlier period, we could not confine our thinking to their concepts, or, indeed, accurately conceive them. And, if we made our characters of any earlier period speak as casually as people always did speak, no one used to the stilted speech of fiction would believe us.

It is a nice tightrope, and few historical novelists have successfully walked it: to use language that doesn't intrude the present while not setting the past at an incomprehensible distance; language that leaves the people of the past without avoidable distortion, yet which never suggest that their only difference from us is one of date; language which sets them naturally and humanly in their own time and environment, without jolting us by archaism or anachronism or apparent improbabilities; language which presents them as nearly and really as people as we are ourselves; language which can do all this and yet is not so neutral as to be colourless, as I fear the language of this talk may be. For I have given it, purely for my own amusement, in language that would have been entirely available to people living in England in the 1880s – with the single exception of the phrase 'three-piece band.'

Bernard Crick

Against promiscuity

'Words, words, words', answered the Lord Hamlet. 'The ball seemed in the net, Montgomery lifted himself off the ground, somehow he got his fingers to it, a miracle, deflected it off the cross-bar; he was there by some supernatural instinct. Words fail me to describe the scene . . . !!' No they blooming didn't, or if so, then only for the briefest moment. He was just getting his breath back. Then out flowed the words again. Never at a loss for words, but sometimes perhaps *homo sapiens*, *ludens*, the Fallen Angel or the Naked Ape is at a loss for the right words.

So I am not so sanguine (which is a lovely word to look up in the full *Oxford English Dictionary*) as Marghanita Laski said she was about the coinage of new words. Yes, indeed, it is one of the glories of our double-rooted English language that with it we can so readily make new words and extend the meanings of others. But they had better be good ones. Since we haven't got a French or a Hebrew Academy trying to steer the language, rather as governments try to steer the economy, and since even Sir Ernest Gowers in his great book, *Plain Words*, was just a little bit up-tight, then it is up to all of us who love the language to be a little sceptical, conservative or preservationist about the coiners and developers. I am wide open to be convinced, but I hate promiscuity with words.

Take just two innocent sounding extensions like 'extremist' and 'dialogue'.

How often is the concept 'religious extremist' used when what is really meant is 'fanatic' or 'zealot', both good old words, someone extreme in his claims or action, but not necessarily the extreme point of a common tendency of the religious. He may be a logical *reducio ad absurdam* of orthodoxy or he may be plain idiosyncratic. But with the common phrase 'student extremist' the tar-brush of extended meaning is often deliberate. In any precise sense 'student extremist' usually refers to either Revolutionary Socialists or to anarchists: but the phrase carries the naughty implication that the extremist exemplifies what is latent in all students – I mean that they are an extrapolation from a rising curve of homogenous student response. If the others were not a right lazy set of bastards, or slackers in a Dr Arnold or Mr Gladstone sense, they would be out there with the 'student extremists' on the streets fighting for liberation against repression, or with them in the teach-ins reifying or deifying the Young Marx (who never grows old). But students are in fact a pretty mixed bunch – I mean are functionally differentiable into a plurality of sub-cultures. If the slackers did pull their socks up, some of them would be out there on the streets, some would be boozing and brawling with the rugby club; some would be swotting and cramming even harder; some of them would be having religious revivals; others would be even nicer than they are now, and some still wouldn't have a clue what they are doing. The so-called extremist is, in fact, more likely to be way-out, isolated and – however righteous – on his own, not the tip of a tendency as the loosely used word implies.

'Dialogue' is a more beautiful but an arrogant word. Can't we just meet and talk together anymore without the salad-dressing of pretence that there will be a dramatised and personified absolute reason confronting, with platonic clarity, such another? 'O Kosygin, consider that we Americans believe that all men are born free.' 'O Nixon, consider that we Russians believe that all men are born equal.' The dialogue between East and West, presumably. But it even creeps into my telephone. 'Bernie, I think you and I must have a dialogue at some approximate date about our emerging points of substantive difference.' Or 'Crick, could you come round to talk to me soon. A quiet word together might be useful at this stage.' Somewhere between overstatement and understatement there must be ways of saying more clearly what the character of a meeting is to be. 'Dialogue' is such a pretentious, trendy, mid-Atlantic *Encounter*-magazine sort of word, either the obvious on well-gilded stilts or else delusive fairy gold.

And when I hear that a 'meaningful dialogue' is promised, then I weep for all the others. I would that I could render dialogue 'inoperative'.

Proper authority

It is said that the Mandarin officials of ancient China believed that the business of good government demanded an official 'rectification of terms': that if every word by imperial edict were returned to its original, precise and distinct meaning, justice and tranquillity would be assured. Such a programme would, indeed, be authoritarian. But I do want, none the less, some proper authority. Simply because there is neither any single original meaning of a word, say like 'authority' itself, nor any single demonstrably correct usage, it is all the more important, not less, that those who are commonly admitted to use words well, and hence are given some slight authority about the usage of words, should not accept that anything goes. Power is useless if it cannot influence people. The Mandarins had the power to order the freezing or reform of language, but it would have had no effect unless people accepted their authority. And it is unlikely that they would have done. Their authority was accepted, presumably, for the business of government, not for the rectification of language. 'Authoritarian' is the abuse of authority. All authority is not authoritarian. Proper authority is exercised by people who are recognised to be skilful in fulfilling a function that is accepted as needed. I have authority, while I am skilful and knowledgeable, as a teacher of my subject; and usually have no difficulty in exercising my authority in relevant ways. But if I use my narrow authority as a teacher of a subject to lay down the law to my students about their morals or about the benificence or iniquity of the Government of the day, then I am abusing that authority and I would expect them to interrupt, switch off or drift away. It is foolish to be against authority as such: but we should always be against the extension of one type of authority, however relevant and good, into other and irrelevant fields. In the same way we should be against the arbitrary extension of the meaning of words which already have burden enough to carry.

So let us not be authoritarian about the defence of our language, particularly since it is now – *pardonnez-moi, messieurs* the new *lingua franca* and used by so many other peoples, but let us not be frightened to use any brief authority we still happen to be dressed in, or else the result may be a cumulative vagueness of meaning, a gradual debasement of language. That is why I, unlike Marghanita Laski, admit to a prejudice against new words. Not intolerance mind, simply initial prejudice. I want to put them through some pretty stiff hoops before accepting them fully. Do they add to clarity, or subtract from it? Do they have a greater resonance, or simply a sloppy vagueness?

If I had authority, if I were King of Words for a day, a word I would specially like to persecute and crack down on is escalation. I knock it out of *Political Quarterly* articles and student essays every time I can catch it. As when people talk about 'the escalation of violence', seeming to mean that a single or a few observed instances of something they don't like is the beginning of an inevitable process of cumulatively horrendous events. Built into escalation is a concept of inevitability and also of things getting out of control, but getting out of control – paradoxically – in a predictable sort of way. Not the 'explosion' of violence, for that is too unique and unpredictable an event, nor a fashionable 'implosion' of violence either, but a full-scale lumbering escalation: a getting worse step by predictable and irresistible step.

Of course, people who use the word are just trying to frighten us or themselves: they never in fact believe that the processes are (as they seem to say) irreversible or irresistible. They are usually meaning to say that if you don't accept quickly my well-meant but arbitrary wonder-cure, so far untested, things will get so out of hand as to remove all possibilities of choice. Well, as a student of society I'm not taking that unless the evidence is put on the table, or unless it is at least admitted that there is time to stand on the same step together and to ask precisely and for what reasons one is thought to be part of this spiral escalator. And doesn't, by the way, an escalator turn round and come down again? The 'middle-class backlash' will then set in just as rigidly as our tired old Marxist friend, 'inevitable reaction'. I wonder if the dialectic can escalate?

Pornography, pollution, drug addiction and violence are nasty and wrong things, but they are simply not escalating, as that other old traditionalist in *The Times* keeps on saying who would do better to defend the tradition of the language itself than to use such words. No, I am not facetiously complacent. Things may get worse if such and such conditions continue, arise or coincide. But to combat them, we must specify them. And to be specific is to see that there are choices of action. 'Escalate' has become as shoddy a blanket concept among the political right as was ever 'inevitable tendencies' among the left. Some degree of graduated de-escalation is overdue.

Only disconnect

It occurred to me that social science jargon has a kind of latent poetry in it:

> Come correlate hypotheses
> And if thou thinkst as I
> We'll soon conceptualize a hunch
> In one subjective sigh.
> Let interdisciplinary zeal
> Now count the feedbacks down
> And spark the old bi-polar urge
> Neath thy conceptual gown.

There are in fact three literary quotations and only three which turn up regularly in the textbooks of social scientists. The first is Yeats's 'Things fall apart, the centre cannot hold' – which can be applied to anything; the second is W. H. Auden's 'Hunger is something which hurts the citizen and the police. We must love one another or die' – which he got so fed up with, presumably because of its glib falsity, that he removed it from later editions of his *Collected Poems*; and, thirdly, of course, E. M. Forster's 'only connect'.

Someone wrote a textbook on British politics with that legend, no names no pack drill, a rose by any other name etc. And the trouble was that he did connect everything. He had a theory about what the essential functions of government are, full of words like in-put and out-put, affect and effect, upon which facts were strung like coloured bulbs on the arms of a plastic Christmas tree. Everything was connected, simply because he assumed that there was a SYSTEM. Now whether everything in British politics and society is related systematically is, you might innocently think a matter of fact, an empirical matter. But no, it turned out to be a theoretical assumption: it was assumed that there was a system. Indeed the word 'model' was used; but the model didn't really claim to be a replica of an actual social system, but rather something like an old-fashioned clothes horse, on which any old country can hang its wet clothes in some kind of order.

Thus 'system' and 'model' can, in the social sciences, either claim that an intellectual framework must be imposed on an otherwise random world of events, or that the world of events consists in fact of mutually consistent regularities. The one sense of system is a tautology, whatever one sets up then is true by definition, but the other is true presumably only if it can be empirically verified. But, in fact, it never is. All we get is words, words, words. How do we form our basic conceptions about politics? By processes of socialisation. Why should we obey the state? To meet the functional prerequisites of mechanisms of legitimation. Do we want different things out of politics? Yes, we are cross-pressured by differential role perceptions. There is better to be found, of course, but there is too much of this kind of thing: purely verbal answers: opium puts one to sleep because it has a soporific quality. As I sit editing an article which may actually have something to say, beneath the ingrained verbiage, and as I try to put nouns back into verbs, passives into actives, and to remove 'isms' and 'isations' from nearly everything, I shudder to think at the amount of congested and unclear writing that the social sciences tolerate, and at their enshrinement of banalities. To write plainly is to be suspect of being merely literary.

Consider the great Yale scholar Harold Lasswell ruminating about content analysis of the word 'democracy':

'Our problem may therefore be posed as follows: Under what conditions do words affect power responses? If we let the "power responses" in which we are interested be referred to by the letter R, the problem is to find what words in the environment of the responders will affect R in one way rather than another, given certain predispositions on the part of the audience (other environmental factors being held "constant").' Tristram Shandy long ago analysed these things more exactly: 'Now there are such an infinitude of notes, tunes, cants, chants, airs, looks, and accents with which the word fiddlestick may be pronounced in all such cases as this, everyone of 'em impressing a sense and meaning as different from the other as dirt from cleanliness — that causists (for it is an affair of conscience upon that score) reckon up no less than fourteen thousand in which you may do either right or wrong. Mrs Wadman hit upon the *fiddlestick* which summoned up all my Uncle Toby's modest blood into his cheeks'.

Plain propaganda

How well I remember my acute embarrassment on first reading George Orwell's great essay 'Politics and the English Language' when, after nodding at every line of the first page with vigorous and amazed delight, I ran into his very first example of combined ugliness of style, tiredness of imagery and imprecision of meaning – coming from the pen as if from the very lips of my late teacher:

> 'I am not, indeed, sure whether it is not true
> to say that the Milton who once seemed not unlike
> a seventeenth century Shelley had not become, out
> of an experience ever more bitter in each year,
> more alien to the founder of that Jesuit sect
> which nothing could induce him to tolerate'.

Harold Laski, of course, alas. And five negatives in fifty-three words, rubs in Orwell. Orwell's essay was, of course, concerned with obscurity of utterance both through incompetence and for deliberate political effect. Now one can defend language against abuse and argue for a plain, direct and lively style in the name of meaning and comprehension or in the name of taste and aesthetics. 'Kind hearts count more than coronets, and Saxon roots than Latin synthesis'. But Orwell was eager to show the precise political advantage of a clear and simple language.

This precise advantage was made more clear in an earlier essay, 'Propaganda and Demotic Speech'. There he wishes, simply or perhaps grandly, 'to bridge the intellectual gulf', he says, 'between rulers and ruled . . . the same gulf which lies always between the intelligentsia and the common man'. His theory of style was indeed part of his doctrine of politics. 'The whole idea of trying to find out what the average man thinks,' he says, 'instead of assuming that he thinks what he ought to think, is novel and wholesome . . . What is wanted is some way of getting ordinary, slipshod, colloquial English on paper'.

But why, one may ask, is this wanted at all? His answer is plain and political: to demonstrate that there is nothing important politically which cannot be explained to ordinary people in ordinary words. But even if 'slipshod'? Here he surely goes too far, and shows that his own socialist arguments have a special kind of rhetoric about them too, not a technical or pseudo-scientific one, such as he mocks so well, but a colloquial rhetoric. Does one by using a colloquial style necessarily understand better the common man? This suggestion can be as dangerous as the rhetoric of pseudo-science. There are dangers in a populist theory of style. Some thoughts of philosophy, religion and social theory are very difficult and are more likely to be misunderstood if put in too homely and conversational a style. To be precise and to be colloquial is not always easy.

Once more he came down like a ton of bricks on the unfortunate Laski who had rashly criticised T. S. Eliot for 'writing only for the few'. What rubbish, says Orwell, to say this 'of one of the few writers of our times who have seriously tried to write English as it is spoken – lines like (he quotes):
'And nobody came, and nobody went,
But he took in the milk and he paid the rent'
although I think Orwell might have conceded that there are lines somewhat less clear in some of Eliot's other poems. 'On the other hand (continues Orwell), here is an entirely typical sentence from Laski's own writing':
'As a whole, our system was a compromise between democracy in the political realm – itself a very recent development in our history – and an economic power oligarchically organised which was in its turn related to a

certain aristocratic vestigia still able to influence profoundly the habits of our society.'

And as the offending sentence came from a printed lecture, asks Orwell, did he actually stand up and spout it forth, parenthesis and all? And the odd thing is that he did. I heard him many many times. And it was very effective. Laski was often above the heads of his audience, but they respected the visible sincerity of this professorial gentleman in trying so hard to explain difficult things to them. Orwell, on the contrary, was a poor platform speaker and indeed an indifferent broadcaster. Perhaps he was too honest to perform those funny tricks one has to do in order to appear even half-way natural. Now I'm not defending Laski's over-rhetorical and over-congested style. But it is easier to be colloquial when attacking the abuse of power, as did Swift, Hazlitt, Cobbett and Orwell himself, than in trying to set out new and positive doctrines and theories. So many of us are deeply affected both by Orwell's style and his politics. But I sometimes wonder if his theory of language didn't doom him to being far more appreciated as a critic than as a positive moralist – as he also wished to be.

Randolph Quirk

Le mot juste

It is often said that, provided you're not in the unfortunate minority of people who have pathological language defects, your language mechanism automatically equips you to say anything you need to say. This doesn't mean that I can talk about all the technicalities of company law or of central heating with the glibness of a solicitor or a plumber; what it does mean is that if my job or my hobby entailed a knowledge of these activities, my language would rise to the occasion. It's rather like Parkinson's law. There's a natural linguistic ecology which dictates that your stock of words expands or contracts according to the demands made on you. As the horse-drawn carriages declined in use, so we lost the need and hence the ability to refer to the differences which eighty years ago were freely expressed by words like phaeton, brougham, or landau. But of course we've balanced such losses with words which distinguish between convertibles, fastbacks, dormobiles and minibuses.

Well, in general, all this is true: any normal person has the language tools to handle anything he needs to handle. But there are odd little exceptions. Take forms of address to strangers. Quite often we need to draw someone's attention to something that's just dropped out of pocket or handbag, or to the fact that someone's just going to walk into a plate glass door. Not merely does English lack anything corresponding

to the French *attention* or German *Achtung*, but we don't have
the equivalent of M'sieur or Madame or even Mademoiselle.
Some people manage very effectively with 'Watch it, mate' or
'Look out, lady' or even 'Hey, missis', but these forms are
outside the range of polite educated usage. We can try
shouting 'Excuse me!' but that's ambiguous: it may be taken
to mean that we just want to push past in a hurry. 'Excuse me,
sir' is awkward unless you're a very young male speaking to
a much older one. 'Excuse me, madam' makes you sound like
a door-to-door salesman – and can hardly be addressed to
a teenage female anyway. By this time, the stranger has
bumped into the plate glass or has disappeared leaving you
to take a fur glove to the police station.

Not long ago, a foreign visitor whose English is extremely
good told me of his embarrassment in a tea shop. He knew
that although you could call out 'Waiter' to a man, you
couldn't call out 'Waitress' if the place was staffed by
women. So he tried Miss and had been forced to cringe by
the large middle-aged married waitress who had turned on
him: 'And who are you calling miss, young feller?'

There are many arbitrary little limitations on our language like this. While we can single out one story or one
yarn from a number of stories, we can't talk about 'a new' or
'an information'. Instead, we have to use a round-about
expression like 'I have another piece of news (or another item
of information) for you'. While under-clothes (informally,
undies) are made up of individual garments, we can't com-
plain to the laundry that they've mislaid one underclo or one
undy. We can ask a chap how many children he has without
going into the specifics of whether they're boys or girls; but
we can't ask him how many brothers and sisters he has
without getting precisely these irrelevant sub-answers and
then totalling them.

Now it's true that in this instance we may use the word
siblings, but the very fact that this word remains largely
in technical health-authority usage despite our recognition of
its usefulness and of our need for such a word, this very fact is
an interesting indication of the way we are largely the help-
less prisoners of the language in general use around us. We

like to think that we create our language as we need it, but in fact the scope for an individual to change things is very limited. Even where there would be widespread agreement that there is a linguistic deficiency, very few communities in the world seem to have settled the means whereby remedies can be agreed upon and adopted.

Let me touch upon one other way in which we are equipped somewhat less than ideally to say what we want to say. I mean the problem of word-finding. We're writing something – or worse – we're in the middle of a conversation and we want to refer to the activity of some people who are doing something together in full knowledge of each other's motives but probably unwilling to disclose these motives to others, perhaps because their activity is harmful to other people's interests. Well, all this is pretty longwinded and I'm still not sure that I've expressed all I wanted to and I'm almost certain there's a single word that says exactly what I have in mind. Collaboration, plotting, co-operation, conspiracy, partnership: I fish around and reject each of these in turn because they either say too much or not enough. It's worrying when we can't find the right word, and it's worrying too that when we find it – in this case, collusion – it has, of course, no obvious relation to the rough paraphrase we started with: it's not as if the word turned out to be 'selfish-secret-work-together'. Finally, it's worrying that when we're struggling to find the 'right' word in this way, there's no systematic method, and no guarantee either that the word exists or that if it does we will inevitably find it.

Can you imagine how worrying it must be for those who, through language disability, can almost never find the word they're hunting for?

Is Mrs Jones primiparous?

Of all the books about words, the type that springs most readily to mind is the dictionary. It used to be said that if a home contained any books at all, the two you could depend on finding were a Bible and a dictionary. Whether or not the ubiquity of the Bible still holds in what are sometimes called these post-Christian days, the widespread ownership of a dictionary certainly does.

Well, there's more to our language than just words, but the classic word-book – the dictionary – seems to many people to be the receptacle for the whole language, indeed to be the symbol of it. There seems to be something comforting about having on one's bookshelf a handy directory to all the words of the language. For that's what we regard the dictionary as being.

Let's take one fairly common place example of the comfortable reliance we place on dictionaries. In the game of scrabble, it's usual for the players to take the nearest available dictionary as the standard for admissible words. If a player forms a sequence of letters we are dubious about, we seize the dictionary and if it isn't in, we say in aggrieved triumph 'There's no such word' – and our opponent has to retreat in the face of this unchallengeable evidence.

Just look a moment at the implications of this. First, there's the assumption that, although we are all free to make up new sentences – in fact although we expect every sentence we hear to have been constructed for that specific occasion – there are big constraints on the individual making up new words as he goes along. Secondly, and despite this, there's the overt acknowledgment that no native speaker, however fluent and educated and well-read, is expected to know all the words of his language. Now there isn't time to say anything more about the first of these two implications but perhaps we can think a little about the second. It's strange in a way, isn't it, that although we learn our native language very early (so that by the age of five we can all use words like dog and door, love and fear and hate and hunger quite correctly and effortlessly) it is strange that an educated man in his fifties should still be able to say, 'I'm afraid I really don't know what such and such a word means; I'd better look it up in a dictionary.' There are at least two important reasons for this. Words are the indices of experience, and since we are liable – if we are

active or lucky – to go on encountering entirely new experiences from the cradle to the grave, we'll equally go on
hearing the words that refer to such new experiences. You
wouldn't think that an educated middle-aged man still had
anything to learn about English four-letter words, but if he is
a solicitor or a shopkeeper, he may well have never moved in
yachting circles and so find himself ignorant of the noun yawl
or the still shorter navigational verb, yaw. This is readily
paralleled among speakers of other languages, but the second
reason probably affects speakers of English especially. It
is the fact that English has basically two types of word – the
familiar homely-sounding and typically very short words like
cat, king, crazy and kiss, and the more learned, foreign-
sounding and characteristically rather long words like
corrugated, carbolic, catechism and chrysanthemum. There
are far more words of this latter type among the half-
million words of English than of the former type, and it is
chiefly these that we start learning relatively late in our use
of English, and go on learning (and maybe forgetting)
throughout the rest of our lives. In fact, one reason why we
may not have come across a particular one of these before is
many of them have meanings which have alternative and
simpler expressions. 'I don't like arguing with him: he
prevaricates' we hear someone say – and we may wonder
what prevaricate means without realising that it's more or
less what we ourselves have always used the verb quibble for.
Again, a man may be forgiven if he doesn't know what is
meant by the question 'Is Mrs Jones primiparous?' – though
he would know perfectly well if the doctor had asked whether
she was having her first baby. And even when we've learnt
such words as convex and concave, we may have difficulty in
remembering which is which.

Such problems can hardly arise in a language that has a
homogeneous lexicon such as German. Although like primiparous, *erstmalig gebärend* is chiefly in formal medical use, its
meaning is quite transparent to any German speaker. This
may mean that we need our dictionaries more than the
Germans do: at any rate it probably makes them more fun
to use!

Sir Bruce Fraser

Is that your own hare?

English is full of homophones – that is, words that sound the same but have different meanings – like Brighton Pier and a peer of the realm.

Homophones are the basis of most puns; but that isn't really their fault, any more than you can blame an architectural horror on the glass and concrete that it's made of. Punning was a very popular form of humour with the Victorians, but it appears nowadays mainly in children's comics and Top People's crossword clues. But it seems to be creeping back, in the titles of articles in the *Economist* and in side-headings in *The Times* Diary. Perhaps it's on the way to becoming a pet hobby of the intelligentsia, like approving condescendingly of pop art or admiring low comedians purely because their timing is so brilliant.

A peer, as I say, has his homophone. So has a knight. So has a baron. And I can give another aristocratic example. In the Scottish peerage there is no Earl of Ayr, and therefore no Countess of Ayr. But when I was in the Scottish Office this mythical lady figured repeatedly and with shattering effect in a letter I dictated about a local road scheme. The shorthand typist couldn't detect the subtle difference between the Countess of Ayr and the County Surveyor. And there's another mythical lady who has puzzled many children in church, when they hear the words 'Surely the good Mrs Murphy shall follow me all the days of my life.'

I don't mean to sound superior about puns. They can be very funny indeed.

Nothing is to be despised in the use of words if it is well done. One needn't approve of the purpose. Some people approve even less of cigarette advertisements or blue limericks or social gossip columns than they do of puns. But whatever their purpose, whether lofty or trivial, lasting or ephemeral, words well chosen and well arranged should get their meed of praise. Words have never been more perfectly chosen and arranged than in W. N. Ewer's famous eight-word epigram, which only a Jew could have written:

> How odd
> Of God
> To choose
> The Jews.

So let us not reserve our applause for the literary giants. Let us salute also, not only the neat epigrammatist and the good punster, but the author of a snappy advertising slogan, the friend who writes a good bread-and-butter letter, the stranger in the street who tells us clearly and concisely how to get to Acacia Avenue (and how rare *he* is!), the sports writer who doesn't indulge in literary airs and graces but just makes us feel that we were there, the television commentator who sets the scene for us as vividly as Richard Dimbleby did.

All these and many other honest craftsmen in the use of words contribute in their different ways to our enjoyment of life, to the quality of our linguistic environment, doing us a service just as manifest as the disservice done to us by those who misuse the language – those, for instance, who inflict on us pretentious and flatulent phrases like 'the quality of our linguistic environment'.

And when these honest craftsmen are at their best, when they can be rated not as mere craftsmen but as artists in the use of words, why then, though they may not realise it, they are in the same company as Shakespeare and Sir Thomas Browne and Jane Austen and Sir Winston Churchill. Some way below the salt, perhaps, and attending the feast perhaps on a day-return ticket, not a permanent passport; but there all the same. I am sure that in an adjoining room David Low and Phil May and Walt Disney quite often take a meal with Hogarth and Dürer and Leonardo da Vinci, and I daresay that the man who first drew Johnnie Walker occasionally drops in too.

This seems to have taken us some way from homophones, with which I started. They led me on to talk of the use of words for trivial or ephemeral purposes. But to be trivial is not necessarily to be ephemeral. Some verbal trivia live on for years, even for centuries, coming up as good as new to each succeeding generation. Even the oldest joke is new the first time you hear it, and even the newest joke is dead if it isn't funny. But I mustn't wander off again from homophones; and we can wind up our study of homophones by recalling, from less than 200 years ago, the well-known story of two fine gentlemen who saw an obvious poacher slinking home with a freshly killed hare. They stopped him. 'Is that your own hare?' said one of them sternly, 'or is it a wig?'

It's magic

When we speak of the magic of words we must beware of making too facile a judgment. Words do indeed have a power in themselves – their meaning, their sound, even their spelling. The force of the word thorough, for example, seems to me to be much enhanced by the way we spell it. When we look at it on the page we catch a glimpse of the great god Thor beating out metal with his rough hammer and making a thorough job of it. Spell it 'thurra', and all this is lost. Some of the magic has gone out of the word. When an earthquake engulfs a city or the rising tide engulfs a child's sand-castle it seems a shame that we no longer use the old spelling 'engulph.' The 'ph' somehow makes the engulphing much more voracious.

But the magic subsists not only in the words themselves but also in their associations. To adulterate the milk and to trespass on another's property both, I think, acquire extra opprobrium from the mention of adultery in the Ten Commandments and of trespasses in the Lord's Prayer. And because sectarian now carries with it associations of violence and bloodshed in Northern Ireland, I don't think we can any longer use it without offence to describe the petty differences between one cosy little school of philosophy and another.

The most striking case I know of a choice of word which proved fatal because of its associations was Neville Chamberlain's choice of appeasement. He described his policy as one of 'general European appeasement', and he meant no more than pacification, a policy of promoting peace in Europe. It must have seemed to him rather a good phrase. But to appease someone carries with it the notion of bowing to force by propitiation and concession. To pacify someone has a bit of the same flavour but not nearly so much, and he might have got away with 'general European pacification'. But appeasement suggested by association a policy not of pacifying Europe but of truckling to Hitler, and that association proved fatal to the phrase.

Words acquire magic too from their setting, from their interaction with other words, from the rhythm and lilt of the sentence, in prose as well as in verse. Macaulay would follow a long, reverberating sentence with a short, sharp one; and the words in the short sentence were suddenly sharper.

Mr Bernard Levin is a good chooser of words, and he has discovered that if he arranges them in long labyrinthine sentences, with parenthesis within parenthesis like the skins of an onion, they somehow acquire an extra quality of humour. And that's magic of a sort, just as Gibbon's rounded sentences or Hemmingway's short ones are magic of another sort.

And for the spoken word there is another source of magic in the way it is spoken – the quality of the voice, the timing and pitch and emphasis and intonation. There is black magic here as well as white. There must have been some black magic, not only in his choice and arrangement of words but in his delivery too, that enabled Hitler to bemuse so many of his decent fellow-countrymen. And for white magic we need go no further than a West End theatre, where a skilful actor or actress will often make silly or phoney dialogue sound like sense and truth – till the curtain falls and the magic is dispersed.

But when we think of the magic of words we needn't come over all high-falutin' and mystical. Words are intended to convey meaning. Some ways of choosing and arranging them have been found in practice to do the job more vividly and accurately than others. And it's because we can't always say precisely why, because what we perceive is more than what we can explain, that we use the rather facile word magic to account for it.

That words can convey meaning at all – that we can actually transfer thought from one mind to another by wobbling our lips and tongues and larynxes, or by making shapes on a bit of paper – even if the thought is no more than 'Go away' or 'I'm hungry' – that is perhaps the real magic of it. And in that sense, whether we are writing deathless verse or telling the children to keep quiet, words do make magicians of us all.

Plobby and wofflesome

English is a marvellously rich language, probably the richest in the history of man. And it gets richer all the time. Science and slang, to name only two sources, add new words to our vocabulary every year. Yet there are still some gaps, where we need a word that we just haven't got.

Sometimes there's a defect in the inflexion of quite common words. 'I'm leaving because I must. I left because I – musted?' No. Musted is a non-word. We can only say 'I left because I had to'. And if you want to bore yourself to tears you can find plenty of other examples in the grammar books.

More often it's a noun, adjective or verb that doesn't exist at all. Either we get on without it, or we import a foreign word – like wanderlust for example. Or else we wait for some brilliant man to invent a new word for us. Let us here pay homage, humble and heartfelt, to Lewis Carroll. But for him chortle would still be a non-word, and galumph and burble and whiffling.

Edward Lear also invented non-words but he was not as successful as Carroll. His chief contribution was runcible, which he applies variously to a spoon, a hat, a cat and a goose but I don't think it met a long-felt want, as galumphing did. True, it has made the dictionaries. Chambers tells me that the phrase runcible spoon has been applied to a broad-pronged pickle-fork. Not by me it hasn't; and if you want to give someone a broad-pronged pickle-fork as a wedding present I don't think you'll get what you want by asking in even the highest-class shops for a runcible spoon.

But it's not only the Victorians who invent non-words for our delight. Witness H. G. Wells' Mr Polly and, to come right up to date, Mr Ken Dodd. Even the majestic genius of P. G. Wodehouse doesn't scorn to have a bash. When that superb pig the Empress of Blandings started feeding again it was with a 'plobby, wofflesome sound'. Elsewhere he describes a character as not actually disgruntled but still far from gruntled. And gruntled is a non-word – or is it? Checking my references I find gruntle already in the dictionary, with a provenance far earlier than Wodehouse. As a verb it means to grunt or keep grunting; as a noun it means a grunt or a snout. It must be disheartening to coin a non-word and find it already in the dictionary – like inventing an ingenious new gadget and then finding it in the local iron-monger's.

But this inventing of non-words is a game anyone can play. For instance, if I described a discussion I had with the producer before he signed me on like this: 'We prabbled along quite lelianly till I asked for more money, and that dis-combubblefusticated him entirely. He krufferbluckled; I snapparteed; things got more and more frounchiant; and we ended up in a proper old grubblescrouch.' Well, I think you'd get a pretty clear impression of how things went. I hasten to add that there's not a word of truth in it. He's a very geniamatic man and there was no grubblescrouch at all.

Children often produce non-words without trying, and parents are apt to bore their friends with their little darling's latest cute invention. Here's one I heard the other day. A small boy was visiting his grandparents. He was bored and said so, adding 'I wish I'd brought my book'. His granny hurriedly produced a child's picture-book, but the little darling just took one look, screwed up his nose and said '*That won't unbore me*'.

Unbore is a non-word, but it ought to exist, oughtn't it? What better word could you or I have used? Amuse, interest, excite, entertain – none of these will do. They all imply lifting from a neutral state to a state of positive amusement, interest, excitement and so on. There just isn't a word for lifting from a state of boredom to a neutral state of – well, of un-boredom.

Christopher Serpell

The female principle

Our linguistic ancestors, the so-called Indo-Europeans, may have been male chauvinist pigs: they certainly traced family descent through the male line, and their sky-god was their father. But when branches of their society pushed into the Mediterranean world down the Greek and Italian peninsulas, they encountered another culture which worshipped the Mother; and after the ensuing mix-up, various aspects of this Mother-goddess had captured influential positions in both the Greek and Roman religions. I came upon the track of these divine ladies when I began to speculate about the origin of our word 'money'. The dictionary told me it came from a Latin word *moneta* which meant the place where the Romans coined their money – the word which also came down through the Old English mynet to give us our mint. But why was the Romans' mint called *moneta?* Because, for reasons unknown, they struck their coins in the temple of Juno, who also had the title *moneta* meaning 'the warning lady'. (You may remember that Latin verb which many of us learnt at school – *monere*, to advise or warn.) And why did Juno get this slightly sinister title? Because, says the Roman author, Cicero, 'on the occasion of an earthquake, a voice came from the Temple of Juno on the Capitol warning the people to purify themselves with the sacrifice of a pig.' It is a mystifying explanation, and one can't help remembering that one of the earliest Roman copper coins carried the effigy of a pig, perhaps to indicate its nominal value. Was Juno perhaps appealing for a subscription? Was her real warning along the lines: 'Because this account is now seriously overdue, we have to advise you etc. etc.'? The guess doesn't seem quite so far-fetched when we find the Romans also used the word *moneta* to translate the name of the Greek goddess of Memory, *mnemosyne* – the name which gives us our *mnemonics* or aids to memory.

So we have a Roman warning lady and a Greek remembering lady, both with their names constructed round the consonants M and N. And they are joined by a third – Minerva, or Mnevra as she was called by the ancient Etruscans who passed her on to the Romans. Oddly enough, Minerva was also associated with a pig in the blunt Roman proverb, 'A pig teaches Minerva' which had the same sense as 'Teach your grandmother to suck eggs'. An ignorant person who tried to instruct his betters was compared to a pig trying to teach the goddess of wisdom or thought. For Minerva was the Roman equivalent of the Greek goddess Athene, who was born out of the head of Zeus and, therefore, symbolised the faculty of intellect or thought. And while we are with the Greeks, we should recall three other very sinister ladies indeed – the three Furies who hunted down those who had broken taboos. To avoid mentioning their awful name too often, the Greeks gave them the title 'Eumenides' – 'The well-intentioned ladies' – in much the same way that our forefathers called the fairies the 'good people'. And once again, in the Eumenides, we find the consonants M and N in the same order; in their case, the name came from a very old Greek word *menos* which came to signify 'will, purpose, or intention'.

So we have no less than four examples of female deities, all with their names or titles built round the letters M and N, and all of them representing some form of mental activity – reminding, remembering, thinking, and intending. And here we have a clue which takes us one stage further back along the trail: the very word mental which comes from the Latin word *mens*, meaning mind, and has an obvious relationship to the Greek *menos*. As you will have noticed, our own word, mind, has the same MN pattern though it comes to us through the Germanic peoples who left the Indo-European heartland by another route. Take a look at some of the senses in which we use the word mind. 'I mind it well', says the countryman when he remembers; 'I have a mind to' indicates his intention; 'mind what I say' is a warning. And when we find that in northern India, the Sanskrit *manas* means mind or spirit, we can have no doubt that the original Proto-Indo-European tongue must have had an MN sound meaning 'to use one's mind'. It is interesting that its speakers when they set out on their migrations should have associated this capacity with the female principle wherever they encountered it. But we mustn't forget one other MN manifestation, the basic word man. Is it just possible this meant originally 'a being who thinks'? Alas, one of my authorities says, 'this very attractive theory is now discredited'. And when you look around the world today, can you really wonder?

Beyond the pale

The old joke about Britain and the United States being divided by a common language was never more clearly illustrated than when the late President Kennedy coined that phrase about 'the new frontier'. To the American electorate, it was meaningful and evocative; to a British audience, it was baffling. For both nations, a frontier meant a boundary or border, but at this point their views of history diverged. To the Englishman, a frontier is a line between nations; he observes it here and there across the Continent, usually marked by a striped pole across the road and an array of customs and passport officials. To the American there has always been only one real frontier – the boundary between settled country and the unknown territories that lie beyond; throughout so much of his history the frontier has been a line that moved progressively westwards – a line associated with pioneers who went beyond and those rugged 'frontiersmen' in their coon-skin caps. So President Kennedy's 'new frontier' implied for his supporters that the spirit of adventure was not dead, that there were fresh fields for American enterprise ahead.

The word frontier comes from the Latin *frons* meaning forehead. It gave the French their front meaning the same thing, while through our Norman ancestors we got front and 'to confront'. The implication is of a head-on encounter and the region where such encounters were likely to take place with the neighbours was named by the French *frontière*. And it was perhaps what Robert Ardrey has named the 'territorial imperative' which has given us so many different words for the line which divides us from the people next door. There was, for example, that peculiarly British boundary, the Pale – the line drawn in Ireland, after it had been invaded by our Norman King Henry II, between the area where British law could be enforced and the tribal territory that lay beyond. A pale is an upright plank of wood, the origin of our park palings, and its use in that context suggests the Normans may actually have tried to keep the wild Irish out with a paling, not unlike the so-called electronic fence which the American forces so hopefully erected against North Vietnam. If fence there originally were, it probably served as useful cover for Irish sharp-shooters, and the line had to be enforced by strong castles until Ireland was completely occupied in Tudor times. But the tradition gave us that uniquely snobbish phrase 'beyond the pale', to designate what Kipling called those 'lesser breeds without the law'. And more English history lies in the phrase 'on the verge'. A verge is a ceremonial rod or wand, like that carried by the verger in church; in medieval England a similar wand of office was carried by the Marshal of the King's Household to denote he had jurisdiction to enforce the King's Peace within a circle of twelve miles' radius from wherever the King's Court might be. Anything that happened within that radius was 'within the verge'; if it was close to the margin, it was 'on the verge'.

Then there was Hamlet's 'undiscovered country, from whose bourne no traveller returns': bourne is a Norman-French version of the word we know better as bounds – a chain of landmarks indicating the limits of a parish or local jurisdiction. It was these bounds that were literally beaten when small boys were escorted round them once a year and caned at key-points to impress on their minds, and other parts of their anatomy, that anything beyond those landmarks was 'out of bounds'.

Finally in landmark we find embedded that ancient word mark or march itself, which appears in the history books in connection with the Welsh or Scottish marches. This word has nothing whatever to do with the armed men who so often marched against each other there; and when a landowner says his ground 'marches' with another estate, it has nothing to do with movement. In all the oldest languages of Europe, versions of mark or march are used to denote a line that divides. Going beyond Europe, the ancient Hittites who were perhaps the first people ever to migrate from the Indo-European homeland, had a verb mark meaning to cut up. In the Holy Roman Empire the Margrave or 'Mark graf' was the count who guarded the marches; in France and Italy the marquis had originally the same duty. Perhaps the strangest version of the word is to be found in Old Norse, the Germanic tongue spoken by the first Scandinavian settlers in Norway and Sweden. For them the word has become *mörk*, and they used it to describe the dark forest-line that lay beyond their clearings. And so we come back to the American conception of frontier, the line between the known and the unknown.

The case of the stranded metaphor

Not so long ago, a BBC news-broadcast about two men trapped in a submarine described them as being 'stranded' some 1300 feet below the surface of the sea; the *Guardian* used a headline 'Stranded in Wet Space' about the same episode. I wonder how many people were struck, like me, by what I should call the illiteracy of this use of the word stranded. It comes, of course, from strand which, ever since the days of the Vikings, has meant the beach, or the sea-shore. Even the old London street which runs from Temple Bar to Charing Cross gets its name because it followed the 'strand' of a tidal river which was much wider before it was confined between embankments. So to strand a ship meant originally to run it ashore or up the beach. Of course, the meaning of the verb has developed since the days of shallow-draught vessels driven by oars; nowadays a ship can be stranded on a shoal or sand-bank. And, in a metaphorical sense, a human being can be stranded in some predicament from which it is not easy to escape.

No doubt it was because this metaphor has become so common – such a cliché – that it was applied to the men in the midget-submarine. What I have called the illiteracy of this application arises because it was used in a nautical context which recalls – or should recall – the original meaning of the word. If that submarine had been really stranded, its crew's plight wouldn't have been so dangerous or dramatic. In fact, it was aground at the bottom of the sea; and there's good precedent for calling the sea-floor 'ground': witness those fishing-grounds which are in dispute off Iceland.

You may feel I'm being unnecessarily precious in making such a fuss about the misuse of a metaphor. After all, a metaphor is by definition the extended use of a word away from its original meaning to a new context; and it is by such extended uses that a language can be enriched. All this is true, but I should argue the enrichment of language by metaphor lasts only as long as we don't absolutely lose sight of the original meanings of the words we use. What gives a metaphor its force or value is the overtones of earlier meaning which vibrate in our memory when a familiar word is used in a new context. But when this metaphorical usage is fossilised into a cliché and all awareness of its origins is lost, then, I maintain, the language is impoverished.

Much of the blame for this impoverishment lies with the news media. Reporters are encouraged by their editors to write what is sometimes called 'bright copy' – reports, that is, which are vivid and stimulating to the public's imagination. Quite legitimately they seek to avoid flat and colourless language which might bore their audience: instead, they would like to borrow from the poet's technique and use evocative words to capture the attention. Unfortunately news material, by its very nature, is produced under pressure of dead-lines; reporters and editors simply haven't got the time to think carefully about the words they use. Instead they snatch out of their memories some alternative to the obvious word, and plug it into their copy merely because it 'sounds different'. Every time they do so, their alternative word loses colour and value because it hasn't been employed with reference to its real meaning. Take the word headache, which in journalese has become the equivalent of problem – 'one of the government's headaches is inflation'. A headache is after all a familiar and sometimes agonising human phenomenon, and nobody imagines that cabinet ministers – and still less, that dreary abstract, the government – suffer from this affliction when they face a problem. But somebody, sometime, used the word 'to brighten their copy'; somebody else borrowed it in a hurry; and now it's become such a cliché that we shall have to misuse some other word, like migraine, to express the sensation of a real headache.

I'm afraid, whatever I or anyone else may say, the process of metaphor-fossilisation will continue. Fortunately there is some compensation in the birth of new words and fresh metaphors in the new fields of human knowledge. But anyone who is involved professionally in the use of words will benefit from becoming at least an amateur in etymology; from the possession, that is, of a dictionary which not only tells you how words are now spelt and what they now mean, but also how they came down to us through the labyrinth of human history.

Kingsley Amis

Sparrow grass and soda water

Like rather too many technical terms in the study of language, 'folk etymology' isn't an ideal expression for what it purports to describe. Let's have a linguist's definition. According to Simeon Potter, folk etymology is the 'substitution of a form with familiar components for one of obscure or less obvious origin', and the example he gives is less famous than it was, probably extinct now: sparrow-grass for asparagus, an old Cockneyism. The process is clear enough: the hearer, not the reader – folk etymologies tend to start among mostly illiterate groups – comes across an odd or difficult word and so to speak domesticates it, making it easier to remember and pass on.

Some of these reshapings drive out the original form and become part of the standard language. A well-known early instance is belfry, which started life in the twelfth century as something like berefraid, became berfrey and barfrey, and then quite abruptly in the fifteenth century turned into belfrey, because that's where you have bells, you see. There's another reason, the tendency of 'r' to change into 'l' if a nearby syllable has also got an 'r' in it, but I think that's secondary.

A fascinating multiple example is avocado, as in pear; I owe my information here to that late lamented other Potter, Stephen, whose study of the origins of English words for plant and animal life, *Pedigree*, I heartily recommend to anyone who likes words and/or plant and animal life. The story of avocado starts with an Aztec word, *ahuacatl*. It means testicle, by the way, and one can catch the allusion by imagining a monorchid scrotum. Well, *ahuacatl* wouldn't do as it stood for the sixteenth-century Spanish invaders of Mexico or their successors. The 'tl' termination had to go. Just as tomatl turned into tomato, *ahuacatl* probably went through a stage of being *ahuacato*, which irresistibly resembled the Spanish word avocado. The fact that it means advocate or lawyer, and that lawyers don't spring to your mind much when you're looking at an exotic tree, didn't matter at all. Avocado wouldn't do for the English at first; until quite recently it was an alligator pear, a good deal more appropriate with its geographical connotations and the sometimes knobbly skin. Alligator itself is a kind of folk etymology, starting life as the Spanish *el lagarto*, the lizard, and ending in the rather posh, Latin and scientific-sounding form we know.

I move now to Jamaica, just the place for this sort of stuff because of the presence of a (regrettably, until recently) large proportion of illiterates who were and are also imaginative. Here the plant supervivium became, rather oddly, simple-bible or single-bible, and the tree poinciana, much more understandably, ended up as Fancy Anna. Place-names, or names for topographical features, are extra susceptible to folk etymology treatment. There's a stream in Jamaica on high ground known as the Wag Water. Originally it was the Spanish *agua alta*, high water. How satisfying that the word meaning water changes into something quite arbitrary and the word meaning high becomes water. Footnote for those interested in sound change: I doubt if *alta* could have turned into water if water had been pronounced in the seventeenth century as it is nowadays. There's a lot of evidence that it used to be watter; the Wag Watter is one more piece of that evidence. There's further evidence (to continue the digression) that the old pronunciation was only driven out in comparatively recent times: Byron wrote, 'I say the future is a serious matter; and now for God's sake hock and soda . . . watter.'

Finally, there are some false folk etymologies round the

place, very common for some reason with the names of pubs. The Elephant and Castle, one of the four London pubs that's given its name to a district, is supposed to have been the Infanta of Castile. No, it originally had a sign showing an elephant with a castle, or howdah, on its back, which was a sixteenth-century use. Then there's the Goat and Compasses – God Encompasseth Us. I don't want to spoil anyone's fun, but can you imagine a man saying to his wife, 'Darling, I'm just popping down to the God Encompasseth Us for a pint with the lads'?

Rightly is they called pig;

'Rightly is they called pigs', said a character in a novel by Aldous Huxley, after a look at life in the sty. The remark was supposed to show him up as a simpleton; in fact, without knowing it he was making a valid linguistic point. The word pig belongs to the class of symbolic forms, as writers on language rather misleadingly call them. Leonard Bloomfield, the great American authority, says: 'Symbolic forms have a connotation of somehow illustrating the meaning more immediately than do ordinary speech-forms'. He goes on to list words that sound rather similar and have a meaning in the same rough area. So some words that begin with the sound 'gl' mean something to do with 'steady light': glow, glare, gloaming, gleam, glimmer, glint. Then, some words ending with the sound 'ump' connect with the idea of clumsiness: bump, clump, chump, hump, lump, stump and several more. Why you get these groupings of sound and sense is a puzzle I won't try to solve now.

Now back to pig. A term of contempt or even loathing, whether applied by an old-style farmer to an animal or by a new-style student to a policeman. That student might care to know, by the way, that that use was first recorded in 1812, only a dozen years after the first policeman appeared in

London. Pig is a monosyllable (therefore emphatic) beginning with the sound 'pi'. There aren't many of those possible in English, but three of them do, or can, carry contempt: pimp, the archaic exclamation pish, and a word very like pish which we all know. A lot of words in the pig group are, let's say, indelicate, therefore showing strong feeling. If we pull back to include monosyllables just beginning with the letter p, the list is much longer: pap, pock, pox, the exclamations pooh and pah, poop (archaic childish term for excrement), pus, poof, poove, ponce, punk (which meant a prostitute in the seventeenth and eighteenth centuries). The sound 'puh', with the puff of breath that goes with it at the beginning of an English word, is tailor-made to express contempt.

Now what about the other end of the word, monosyllables with a short vowel ending in g? Again, a large number convey contempt, some of them indelicate again and several of them slang: bag, cag, drag, fag, slag, nag (a decrepit horse), shag, hag, dreg, prig (archaic slang for a thief), frig, bog, wog, quag (mire), bug (in two senses), slug, mug (in two senses), smug. And when we meet Silas Wegg in *Our Mutual Friend*, we know at once he's up to no good. Of course, there are plenty of -ag and -eg words that aren't derogatory: tag, leg and especially dog, but even that *can*, or could, be used contemptuously.

Finally, the special, restricted cases: monosyllables beginning with p and ending with g. There aren't many possible ones, and most of them aren't words at all; there's no pag as far as I know, no pog. In fact, apart from pig itself, only two exist in the language. Pug isn't contemptuous when applied to a breed of dog, but pug-nosed is offensive, to call a boxer a pug is offensive (never mind its supposed derivation from pugilist), and at various times the word has meant an ape, a dwarf and, as before, a prostitute. The other one is peg, pretty innocuous on the face of it, but it was once used as a verb meaning to gorge or overeat, so I think I score half a mark there. A historical note: pig meaning the animal began to drive out the older word swine in the early nineteenth century, meaning an unpleasant human being ten or twenty years ago.

All in all, if you'd been commissioned to run up a word conveying emphatic contempt on the brink of downright loathing, I can't see how you could have done better than the word commonly applied to *porcus domesticus* and persons regarded as being of the same moral and spiritual status. So absolutely rightly is they called pigs.

Him kerosene blong Jesus Christ

Affee yu sayee yu hadda, ta yu buy hattee, pa yu, pottee ang? Or if you like, if you sell your head, then you buy a hat, where do you put it? – a vivid warning to the reckless. Both those sentences are in English, but the first one was in pidgin English, or rather, in one of its many forms. These dialects are still spoken by millions of people in widely-separated parts of the world, in New Guinea and the former Malay States, in West Africa, in parts of the Caribbean and in the Chinese seaports (though that one must be on the point of extinction). There was an Australian version used between the English settlers and the aboriginals, and a North American Indian one to be heard in old-style Westerns: 'me heap big chief' and so on. They all differ a great deal among themselves, but they have features in common.

The grammar is a very simplified and eccentric form of English; the vocabulary is roughly not very educated early-eighteenth-century English plus a number of words from the local language that the English trader or colonist or missionary put himself to the trouble of learning; the pronunciation is heavily influenced by the local language, so, for instance, the Singapore pidgin for ice-cream is ice-a gullim, and, even more strikingly, the word pidgin is a Chinese attempt to say business. Business English is, of course, what it was mostly about in the first place, but today lots of the locals use pidgin among themselves.

All forms of language deserve to be taken seriously, in the sense that they're perfectly adequate modes of communication, but it's no use denying that some pidgin words and phrases sound rather quaint to our ears. Robert Graves tells the story of the Englishman in West Africa who learnt that an eclipse of the sun was coming up and asked his head boy to explain the situation to the other lads to reassure them in advance. The explanation went like this: 'Him kerosene blong Jesus Christ bimeby all done, bugger up, finish'. Not all that reassuring, I should have thought. You can see part of the same thought-process at work in the pidgin for helicopter, which is 'mixmaster blong Jesus Christ'.

South-East Asian pidgin calls a piano a 'bokkis' – they can't say box – 'bokkis you fight him, him call out'. In the same area, fish and chips is described as 'one piecey swim-swim, now you fly him (fry him), now potatoes'. If you're ordering for your wife as well as yourself, of course, it's 'two time one piecey swim-swim'.

English isn't the only language to have given rise to pidgin forms. Other colonising nations have produced their own versions: Portuguese, Spanish, Dutch – Afrikaans has some pidgin features – and French. They differ just as widely from the standard language: the Haitian for 'he is taller than I' is 'li pi gran pasé mwen' (n denotes nasalisation), 'il est plus grand passant moi'. By the way, when you next hear a Frenchman boasting about the superiority of his language, tell him this: French is a pidgin Latin that became creolised, that's to say it drove out the local speech, which was a branch of Celtic, and established itself as the *native* tongue of what is now France, minus parts of Brittany, plus parts of Belgium, Switzerland, Canada, etc. It's a chastening thought that the language of Racine and Voltaire and Mallarmé started life when a probably illiterate Roman legionary tried to buy a dozen eggs from an ignorant barbarian in the third century BC. You can finish your Frenchman off by telling him that, although English has adopted more foreign words than any other language, which is why it's so incredibly rich, its grammar and whole structure is home grown.

Ian Grimble

Of all sciences the monarch

Milton spoke of the written word as a sort of legacy to posterity, a posthumous fortune if you like – 'embalmed and treasured up to a life beyond life.' Poets have been particularly apt to dream of this treasure they were hoarding up: like the little saint, Theresa of Lisieux, dreamed of the store of grace she was building up by being good, until she would be able to send it all fluttering down from heaven like rose-petals after she was dead for the help and comfort of others. Poets who were neglected and starving warmed their hearts with thoughts of the immortality their words would give them. John Keats, dying of consumption, feared only that he would not live long enough to pour out his treasure of words.

> When I have fears that I may cease to be
> Before my pen has gleaned my teeming brain,
> Before high pilèd books in charactery
> Hold like rich garners the full-ripened grain. . .

Keats had to believe there was something special about the way *he* used words – otherwise it wouldn't have mattered who filled the garners with full-ripened grain. And he was said to have been made iller by a critic of his poetry who didn't share his own high opinion of it. In fact the poor reception his poetry got in his lifetime was thought to have hastened his death, so that Byron remarked:

Tis odd, the soul, that very fiery particle,
Should let itself be snuffed out by an article.

Byron, who could use words like fork-lightning, had the greatest contempt for the pedlars of pulp literature, and couldn't understand why Keats, who was spinning words for posterity, should have bothered over what a hack reviewer had to say about them. But it was all very well for Byron. While hardly anyone read Keats during his lifetime, Byron was a best seller and people said he was the greatest poet in Europe. He was even driven to remark that some of it was over-valued and wouldn't stand the test of time.

What did he mean exactly? So far as words are concerned, what makes a single diamond or a cluster of precious stones, or gold or silver? A totally forgotten poet wrote: 'I dreamt that I dwelt in marble halls.' I doubt whether anyone knows his name or a single other line of poetry he wrote. Yet he had that dream and put it in eight words that have not been forgotten. And it shows how it isn't really just words that fill the garners with full-ripened grain but the thoughts of the mind and the feelings of the heart that they express, so compellingly that for ever or for a long time they will move other minds and hearts. This is what distinguishes them from the words that fill the dustbins of pulp literature.

Look at the words in which Shakespeare set out (quite self-consciously) to give immortality to an object of his affections – a young man as it happened.

But thy eternal summer shall not fade
Nor lose possession of that fair thou owest,
Nor shall death brag thou wanderest in his shade
When in eternal lines to time thou growest.
So long as men can breathe, or eyes can see,
So long lives this, and this gives life to thee.

And so long is now nearly 400 years. But it's the words that have lasted: we don't even know for certain whom Shakespeare was talking about. His name has fared no better than the name of the girl which his contemporary Edmund Spenser wrote in sand.

> One day I wrote her name upon the strand,
> But came the waves and washèd it away.
> Again I wrote with a second hand,
> But came the tide and made my pains his prey.

More words that have survived for nearly 400 years longer than the person they commemorate. As the starving poet in his garret knew, it was not the rose nor Helen's beauty that gave immortality to what he wrote about them, but the magic he conjured out of words. And the contemporary of Shakespeare and Spenser, Sir Philip Sidney, put it in a nut-shell when he wrote: 'Now therein of all sciences is our poet the monarch. For he doth not only show the way, but giveth so sweet a prospect into the way as will entice any man to enter into it. He cometh to you with words set in delightful proportion. And with a tale forsooth cometh he unto you, a tale which holdeth children from play, and old men from the chimney corner.' And surely the way Sir Philip Sidney illustrates what he is saying by the way he puts those words together is at least as effective as the argument they contain.

Poet's corner

Well over two thousand years ago Euripides gave a piece of advice to mankind in one of his plays that might have gone a long way to cure human greed and discontentment if only more people had lived by it. 'Enough,' said Euripides, 'is as good as a feast.' Very few people understand the language of Euripides any more, or know that it was he who uttered those tremendous words so long ago, or have the sense to take his advice. And it's something of a miracle that the play in which Euripides first used those words has survived, be-cause of the 92 plays he wrote, we only have 18 and some fragments today.

Would his precept have been remembered – and ignored –

down the centuries if the play in which it appears had been lost? Would it have stood a better chance if it had been carved in stone? This was what the great Indian emperor Asoka did with the precepts of Buddha, less than two hundred years after the death of Euripides. He had them carved on stone pillars so that people would be reminded of them throughout his realm – and you can still see Asoka's pillars throughout India, over two thousand years later. On the other hand, the precepts of Buddhism have not needed the durable qualities of stone to preserve them, while most great rulers and conquerors like Asoka have carved words in stone for the very different purpose of giving immortality to themselves – and that hasn't always worked. You may remember the great broken pedestal in the empty desert that Shelley wrote about:

> And on this pedestal these words appear –
> 'My name is Ozymandias, King of Kings.
> 'Look on my works, ye mighty, and despair.'
> Nothing beside remains. Round the decay
> Of that colossal wreck, boundless and bare,
> The lone and level sands stretch far away.

How Shelley would have laughed at some of the monuments in the poets' corner of Westminster Abbey. But not all of them. Byron was refused burial there because his writings or his life or both were considered too immoral: but recently he has been allowed a plaque in the floor inscribed with his own lines:

> But there is that within me which shall tire
> Torture and time, and breathe when I expire.

I think he would have approved of the choice. And nearby there's another stone in the floor with T. S. Eliot's name on it, and the quotation chosen from his writings is this: 'The communication of the dead is tongued with fire beyond the language of the living.' The dream of every starving or neglected poet – though T. S. Eliot himself was neither of those. And what did they choose from the words of Edmund Spenser, who wrote his lover's name in the sand, and left all those thousands of lines of *The Faerie Queene* to choose from? Nothing. They leave the choice to you, with the recommendation that Spenser was 'the prince of poets in his time, whose divine spirit needs no other witness than the works which he left behind him.'

The plaque on the wall that carries this inscription is dwarfed by a great memorial to Mathew Prior with portrait bust and yards of eulogy in Latin. Who reads this Latin today, or anything Mathew Prior wrote in English for that matter? And what about John Milton, the poet who was such a great Latinist himself? A modest plaque on the wall informs you in English merely that he wrote *Paradise Lost* – not *Paradise Regained* or anything else. Because the available space is filled mostly with information about the people who erected the monument. What a seemly contrast is the epitaph to Ben Jonson, who actually saw Shakespeare performing as an actor. We know that an admirer of Ben Jonson ordered a mason to carve over his grave in the abbey 'O rare Ben Jonson' and we know this despite the fact that the admirer and the mason had better taste than to carve their own names there as well.

And what about the memorial to Shakespeare himself, the man who wrote:

> Not marble, nor the gilded monuments
> Of princes shall outlive this powerful rhyme?

Is that inscribed on his memorial? No, it isn't, nor anything else he wrote. And the full-length figure of Shakespeare on it is overshadowed on either side by guess whom? Why, James Thomson and Thomas Campbell. And in case you should wonder why their marble figures dwarf Shakespeare's, why the Brontës and Jane Austen are merely names on little plaques behind, and Campbell and Thomson's fellow Scot merely a head peeping out behind with the single word 'Burns' written beneath it, you have lines and lines of their verse to inform you on their pedestals. To which I think Shelley might have added:

> Look on my works, ye mighty, and despair.

Two kinds of arrow

One of the most striking memorials to a man's love for his fellow human beings is the statue of Eros in Piccadilly Circus. It commemorates Anthony Ashley Cooper, who became 7th Earl of Shaftesbury – hence Shaftesbury Avenue which runs down to Piccadilly. Shaftesbury was one of the great Victorian philanthropists and spent his political career fighting for causes like the limitation of working hours in factories, improvement of conditions in coal mines, and the establishment of schools for London children. Philanthropy, a word deriving from the Greek, and meaning love for one's fellow human beings. And Eros himself, that winged youth with his bow and arrow on the Shaftesbury memorial, is the Greek God of love.

But now I've used the word love twice, in the context of two quite different Greek roots – the first the philanthropic one, the second the erotic one; and I'm sure I don't need to spell out the difference. Eros was the son of the Greek goddess Aphrodite, from whom we derive the word aphrodisiac – meaning a drug which promotes sexual desire. And her son Eros accomplished the same object with the bow and arrow which you can see him carrying in Piccadilly Circus. A place where there are generally a fair number of people hanging around waiting to be shot at. But surely this wasn't the sort of love which the 7th Earl of Shaftesbury felt for coal miners or slum children? No, it wasn't. His love was a philanthropic one – one for which the Greeks had a word which they used to distinguish it from erotic love – the word *agapae*. So far as I know, in all our borrowings from the rich language and profound thought of the Greeks, *agapae* was overlooked.

And what about the second language and civilisation to which we owe so much, those of Latin and the Romans? In Latin Aphrodite becomes Venus and her son Eros is Cupid. Hence venereal disease and cupidity, which is another word for lust. It almost looks as though the English had a passion for piling up its vocabulary about erotic love and didn't think *agapae* worth finding a word for. Well, they had to when the Bible came to be translated into English and scholars were faced with the famous epistle of Saint Paul to the Corinthians, the one in which he defined *agapae*. And how did the authors of the seventeenth-century version translate that word from the Greek? 'Charity suffereth long and is kind. Charity envieth not. Charity vaunteth not itself, is not puffed up' – and the definition which goes to the heart of it. Charity 'seeketh not her own.'

So there you see two dramatic consequences of the fact that the immense vocabulary of the English language contains no word for the *agapae* which Saint Paul was defining to the Corinthians, and which Shaftesbury tried to put into practice in his public life. So in the Bible it was called charity, and in Piccadilly Circus symbolised rather differently by the erotic god. Revised versions of the Bible do substitute the word love for charity – for want of any word to define what kind of love. And there's the legend that Cupid has two kinds of arrows, ones with golden heads to implant virtuous love in those they strike, and ones with leaden heads for erotic love. But the gold-tipped arrows are for making you keep your marriage vows. They don't implant the Greek *agapae* as Paul explained it to the Corinthians.

Speech created thought, said Shelley. Let's see how Shakespeare got round what seems to me perhaps the most extraordinary hiatus in the English language, in the play he wrote about love, *A Midsummer Night's Dream*. When he came to the protestation of true love between his young runaways, he very sensibly fell back on the golden-headed arrow of Eros to define what he was talking about. (Though he committed the gaffe of making them call him by the Latin name of Cupid, although they were Greeks, talking in Athens).

I swear to three by Cupid's strongest bow;
By his best arrow with the golden head.

But the play isn't only about the affections of young people, virtuous or otherwise. It also defines love as the loyalty of children to their parents and subjects to their princes. The Duke of Athens says of his less articulate subjects:

> Love, therefore, and tongue-tied simplicity,
> In least speak most, to my capacity.

That isn't erotic love, even with the golden arrow head. It isn't the Greek *agagae* either, which you might not expect to find in this play at all. But consider the blessing of Oberon, King of the Fairies, on the marriage beds of the three newly-weds:

> To the best bride-bed will we,
> Which by us shall blessèd be.
> So shall all the couples three
> Ever true in loving be.

Is that just the gold-tipped arrow again, or has the ambiguity of the English word love enabled Oberon to bestow on those lovers the supreme blessing of *agapae*, on the very night in which it would probably have seemed least important to them?

The measure of the universe

Shelley had this to say about the gift of words that the creator of all things has bestowed on the human species:

> He gave man speech, and speech created thought,
> Which is the measure of the universe.

'Speech created thought.' I imagine a few musicians and artists might take issue with that. But I suppose it's true to say that the overwhelming majority of people have always thought in words. Of course some people who have an exceptional facility with words are not endowed with a corresponding capacity for thought, and no amount of juggling with words can give it to them. A host of minor poets and other writers and successful politicians leave a trail of verbose evidence that this is so. And on the other hand there are lots of people with a real capacity for thought that has to fight for expression with a totally inadequate stock of words.

You might think that this defect is generally due to illiteracy, since it's by reading that most of us have enlarged our vocabularies from childhood upwards. I remember the *obiter dictum* in a famous law case in which a woman had been injured on a railway and had sued the company for damages. The company argued that on the back of her ticket were words which exempted them from liability. The woman's case was that she couldn't read and therefore couldn't be bound by a condition she knew nothing about when she boarded the train. 'Illiteracy,' said the judge, 'is a misfortune, not a privilege'. And the woman lost her case. But although that may have been good law, I think it's an over-simplification of the facts of life. Surely whether you can read and write or not is of secondary importance compared with *what* you read. People who can't read at all may develop far greater powers of original thought than those whose minds are a rag-bag of half-digested opinions from evening papers and colour supplements.

Sometimes they have a large vocabulary of words too, and outstanding skill in using them. But before the invention of the tape-recorder their art in using words was generally lost like a flashing meteor as soon as it hit the ground. And others with this gift, who can also write fluently, still can't invoke the magic of words on paper as they can when they talk. Over twenty years ago I remember describing some experiences I had had in the Navy to a BBC producer, and he said: 'do write a script about them.' So I did and he read it, and said: 'but this isn't how you spoke at all. We can't broadcast this. Come and record what you told me before, and I'll have it typed out as a script.' When we'd done this and I read the script I was appalled. It was the first time I had seen the way I talked written down, and on paper it looked awful.

Actually there's comparatively little provision for any difference between the spoken and the written word in the English language itself – compared, say, with the Japanese language. But remembering my own failures as a broadcaster and author to pay sufficient heed to such differences as there are, I am all the more impressed by those who have little practice in either speaking or writing, and can yet force clear and incisive thought – their very voice, on to paper. For instance, the following passage was written by an 18-year-old with a limited stock of words and no practice at writing, in solitary confinement in a Borstal.

'This is about my life as I know it and remember it from as far back as it goes until the age of seven or eight. There is much that I cannot remember and much I do not know, but I have wrote most of what I can remember. I have often sat and just thought back of my younger years. Sometimes it was very hurting. I have always wished to write about it but up till now I have found it very hard to do so; even now it is not very good but I have done it.'

Actually it is very good indeed, and an interesting feature of it was the phonetic spelling, which preserves in writing the speech of someone whose idiom and accent hasn't been undermined by the standardising influence of the media of mass communication. And I think this is another of the compensating advantages that people enjoy if they have been denied the benefits of a high standard of literacy. A lot of people seem to imagine that there's some sort of social slur implied in not using the standard speech of today, as though it's a sign that they are not so well educated. Well, better educated or not, words spoken in standard English are not necessarily expressing more graphic or profound or clearer thought. Anyway, standard English is constantly changing. Chaucer didn't write:

When that April with his showers sweet
The drought of March hath pierced to the root.

And he wouldn't have been such a good poet if he had. He wrote:

> Whan that Aprille with his shoures soote
> The droghte of March hath perced to the roote.

Very non-u.

John Vaizey

That particularly Cambridge voice

As I always say what I mean, but I don't necessarily mean what I say, I expect other people to be that way too. It took me a good many years to cotton on to the fact that I was always being introduced at meetings as a provocative speaker, and that when I stopped the chairman thanked me for my 'refreshing frankness.' I only wanted to state facts. Not to be provocative. What they meant, it turned out, was that I was bloody rude. I'm not by nature rude, being a somewhat timid man, and genuinely sympathetic to other people, especially if they are what is euphemistically known as 'disadvantaged' – that is, older, iller, poorer or dimmer than I am. But I've found out painfully that my tendency to refreshing frankness causes great annoyance, especially to Americans and to psychologists (both oddly enough groups I have to live with). They are used to having things wrapped up pretty softly so that they don't have hard edges.

The notion that people ought to agree is a fairly common one. The idea is that people of good will can come to an agreement about basic matters. Sometimes that is true. But often it is not. Frequently there is a fairly basic disagreement between people. Your consensus man is concerned to obscure this. But the Cambridge man is concerned to point out exactly where the differences lie. And that's what causes the trouble.

The cause of offence, once traced, is easy to define. I share it with many other people who like me have been helped and handicapped by a Cambridge education. The emphasis there, you see, is on the tersely written word. In my time we had to write a lot every week. And what we wrote was never praised but always criticised. The Puritan reasoning behind this is plain to see. If you were handicapped – foreign, or stupid – your ideas would be of no interest. They would be passed over in silence, or with a few meaningless words of praise and a glass of sherry. But if you were to be taken seriously, then to be taken seriously was praise enough. To be treated as an intellectual equal was the greatest praise that could be given to you. That was silently understood. What was necessary, in an intellectual equal, was to eradicate error and it was to that ruthless task that my teachers set their hand. 'Christ almighty', my supervisor would sigh at the end of my first couple of sentences, and then a lucid but devastating criticism would be delivered, extended in scope, tersely expressed and utterly logical. The effect of this upon the psyche is bracing. The effect on the intellect is to sharpen it up. And it leaves its marks upon your prose style. It makes you incapable of making your meaning obscure. You feel hell-bent, literally, upon some task of intellectual sanitation, slaving to get the nation's ideas sparkling away, when you spot something that you care about that's gone wrong.

Now, this is not calculated to win friends because most people don't make the unspoken assumption that the only reason you are tearing into them is because you think they and their notions are worth saving. They tend to assume that you are being rude on purpose. And as your rudeness is delivered in that particularly Cambridge voice, pitched slightly above its natural level, with odd intonations on certain vowels and words, there is a social class problem as well. They think you are talking down to them. Permanently surprised at the hostility my friendly frankness brings, I am less surprised that hardly anybody from Cambridge does well in politics. Except Stanley Baldwin, and he did badly at Cambridge.

The man in the white coat

Part of my honeymoon was spent in Texas, a somewhat conservative as well as a very hot place. People were almost unnaturally sympathetic to my wife, I thought. Admittedly I was English, but that was really no worse than being from New England, in their eyes. It later turned out that when asked what I was, my wife said an 'economist', and as she swallows her vowels, they jumped to the conclusion that I was a Communist. In the circumstances they were exceptionally hospitable and forbearing.

But to be misunderstood in some simple basic way is the common lot of people who do economics. This is because the words that we use have two meanings – their common-or-garden one, and the specialised one. In the profession – now there's a pretentious thing to say, because of course we aren't a profession, as we don't have a register you can be struck off – as economists, then, we tend to retreat pretty quickly from using words into using mathematical symbols. Now, if you manipulate mathematical symbols it's fairly easy to get the right answers but to ask the wrong questions. A question posed algebraically isn't often self-evidently absurd unless it has an inner incoherence. But the symbols stand for things – for people, or usually groups of people, or collections of commodities, like electric light bulbs, and wheat, and rolls of paper. And, after all, economics is supposed to be about what happens in the world, things like the latest rail strike, or the shortage of oil, so that in the end the words or symbols have to have some correspondence with reality. It's there that the trouble comes, because in the real world words change their meanings. You can't go around all the time saying that you, as an economist, have decided to use a word to mean one special thing, and that alone, even though everybody else uses the word more loosely.

This is a perennial problem with the specialised jargon of those who want the world to think that they are scientists, or the guardians of some esoteric mystery, but who at the same time want to influence public affairs. I once knew a man who was a psychologist. He was very keen to prove that he was a scientist. Every day, when he settled down to read a book or write an article he put a white laboratory coat on, and that made him a professional. It's the same with the language. Specialists try to keep their jargon specialised. What usually happens, I suspect, is that the meaning that we professionals assign to words in fact gradually changes, and loses its precision and subtlety. Take the words 'growth of the national income'. This has a precise meaning. It is that the total volume of goods and services increases from one year to another. It could be that people choose to use the potentiality for more production by working less, and taking more leisure. But gradually, inexorably, the concept of growth, and of the national income, has come to mean (in economics) what it now means in ordinary life, the accumulation of material goods till they are submerging the earth in a great heap of overpackaged rubbish. So, to say that you are in favour of growth, is to sound terrible, as though you want the planet to wallow in a tide of plastic throw-away objects. But economic growth as we conceived it was once rather a noble ideal; it was that odious toil would be replaced by a careful sensitive balance of useful work and healthy recreation.

Bloody Hungarians

One of the most irritating moments in my life was having an article I'd written rewritten. It was when I was in Paris working for an international organisation. I put a lot of work into that article, getting the ideas straight, and setting it all out in order. When it was done I felt modestly pleased with myself. Words and ideas are my job, and I feel very workmanlike about them. So to get my carefully worked out text back, all altered, was a particular affront. Imagine a carpenter making a door, with all the joints carefully grooved, and everything flush and straight, and finding some amateur had set about it with a fretsaw to 'improve' it. He'd do his nut.

The idiot who set about my prose had telescoped sentences, and fused paragraphs together. He had also altered the words. I was brought up on the old-fashioned idea that Anglo-Saxon words are better than Latinate words, when you have a choice. The editor, for that's what he was called, had carefully substituted Latin words for Anglo-Saxon ones throughout my piece. 'Approximately' for 'nearly', that sort of thing. As a result, of course, he had changed the sense, changed it utterly, and far from a terrible beauty being born (as the poet Yeats put it), the result was a lot of jargon-ridden rubbish, full of obviously incorrect arguments badly expressed. Not something to be proud of.

Then I met the man who had done it. The English editor's job was to rewrite the English texts submitted by staff members whose native tongue was Finnish, or Dutch. He was himself, of course, Hungarian. I say 'of course' because in my experience the odds are better than average that people in jobs like that are Hungarian. The editor, whose real job it was to rewrite the drafts from Bongo-Bongo land, was a thorough man, and he therefore rewrote everything that was written in English in the organisation. If a Prayer Book had appeared in his in-tray he would have rewritten the Lord's Prayer. (Indeed, now I mention it, I wonder whether he did have a hand in the New English Bible.) The fact that a piece of prose was by an Englishman, and he was Hungarian, never seemed to him to be a reason for not doing his job.

And, oddly enough, he had a point because the kind of English that is used in international organisations is of a very special kind. It contains no jokes, and it is not colloquial, or Anglo-Saxon. Mr St John Stevas, for instance, as the Minister for the Arts, caused great trouble for the interpreters when he referred to a splendid banquet given in Bucharest by the Romanian government, which would have the effect of making future banquets seem like 'wine and cheese parties'. These parties seem to be as intranslatable as they are disgusting. So international organisations use a lot of special terminology, partly technological and partly American in origin. And since both these ways of speaking – the technological and the American – are heavily dependent upon the kind of English spoken by successive German emigrants to the United States, international organisations use a special kind of Teutonically heavy English. Which is why, when we go to these conferences, we have to translate our thoughts into a new language, internationalese, and why that bloody Hungarian was quite right to alter my English.

Paul Bailey

Sprechen Sie Geordie?

Living in the North East of England, as I have been for the
last two years, is a bit like being in a foreign country: they
say things differently there. I am a Londoner, accustomed to
calling a sparrow by its proper name, but in Newcastle-on-
Tyne this bird is a 'spuggy'. London sparrows often look
dirty, and their Geordie cousins aren't noticeably cleaner:
hacky mucky spuggies are a common sight. In the south,
children eat sweets, or sweeties, but on Tyneside it's bullets
they devour. An apt word, it occurs to me, for those deadly
little objects which ensure that the toothy of today will be the
dentured of tomorrow. Newcastle children, visiting the
seaside, don't paddle, they plodge; a nice word, that, sug-
gestive of mud and messiness. I realise now that when, as a
boy, I went to Southend I didn't paddle, I plodged.

In Newcastle, familiar words take on different meanings.
Dad, for example, is a verb meaning to beat or to beat a mat;
bait is a packed meal, and when people bubble they cry. If a
southerner describes a person as canny, he is indicating that
he or she is cautious, or even cunning, but in the North East
the word signifies approval: a canny man is someone to be
respected.

Ganzie, neb, cuddy, nettie, lowp, hoy-oot: Sprechen sie
Geordie? Nein? Well, nobody's perfect. When I first arrived
in Newcastle, I might as well have been in Patagonia for all

the sense I made of the conversations I heard in pubs and shops. I was particularly disconcerted by the way in which the women called each other man : very Biblical, very basic.

The Geordie pronunciation added to my confusion. I am assured that it is correct Anglo-Saxon to pronounce the word bread as breed, but it does make for confusion. What I cannot accept, however, is gerra for get. The word isn't spelt with two r's and an a, so why say it like that? At the risk of sounding patronising, I can tolerate hacky mucky and all the other words I've mentioned but I do find gerra downright ugly. But then, I find the present conspiracy at Broadcasting House to change secretary into sekkerterry and February into Febooerry equally off-putting. Quaint words are one thing : the mispronunciation of the ones most of us use in everyday discourse quite another. The habit of adding syllables to words ending in 'ling' is becoming very common : strugg-a-ling. Try adding that 'a' to struggled and you'll see how nonsensical it is.

Having said that, I must admit that I'm inconsistent on the subject of pronunciation. The fact that I'm not annoyed when a Cockney says tomorrer may have something to do with my having been brought up in a part of London where Cockney, so to speak, was spoke. Why is it that the Birmingham accent sends me to my private wailing wall? I don't really know; certainly, neither Geordie nor Scouse grates on my ear in the same way. I'm just as inconsistent – and I suspect that most people are – about words : having admitted that I find plodge apposite, why is it that goodies is totally unacceptable to me? I came across it in a poem recently and was horrified.

Many a commonsensical, down-to-earth, plain-spoken northerner has told me that I speak in a posh accent. I am convinced that I do no such thing : I like to think that I speak the language I love correctly and with some measure of respect for its beauty. God forbid that I should ever talk posh. Some years ago, I worked in the magazine department of the well-known store in Knightsbridge. A young woman came in one day and asked for something called Flah. 'I beg your pardon?' I asked. 'Flah,' she insisted, 'Flah.' 'I'm sorry,' I said, 'I've never heard of it.' 'Of course you have; it's very populah: Flah.' 'Flower?' I inquired, picturing some obscure horticultural journal. 'No, no, no– Flah. FLah!' Then it dawned on me: 'Oh, you mean Flair.' 'That's what I said all along– Flah.' I told her the magazine would be in the following day. She duly turned up. 'Thah,' she said, handing me the money. Let me assure my friends in the North that that is what we in the South mean by talking posh. The language of Belgravia is not the one we speak hyah, thah and everywah.

Getting it straight

Nearly forty years ago, Emlyn Williams wrote a play called *He Was Born Gay*. Williams's hero was a man 'disposed to joy and mirth' and 'addicted to social pleasures and dissipations'. He was, in a word, gay. If he was a homosexual, then that was an aspect of his personality which Williams chose not to reveal. In the 1920s, Noël Coward composed a song with the title *Let Our Affair be a Gay Thing*, by which Coward meant 'let our affair be light-hearted, exuberantly cheerful, sportive and merry'. But being a man of few words, he preferred to write 'Let our affair be a gay thing'.

Times have changed since those days; the days of *The Well of Loneliness*. I'm very glad the times have changed, and that hundreds of thousands of men and women can live out their lives in an atmosphere of tolerance and acceptance. Despite the braying of that vociferous minority, this is a tolerant age we live in. I think it's true to say that a book like *The Well of Loneliness* – so ungay, so portentous, so defensive – could not be written today. We now know, thank God, that homosexual women are not necessarily tragic victims on whom nature has played a dirty trick, but ordinary human beings who are even known to smile on occasions.

But I do deplore the fact that the word gay has taken on a

new meaning. Of course, the meanings of words change, and it is right that they should: nevertheless, this is one change I don't like. I'll explain why. First of all, the choice of gay for homosexual seems to me to help perpetuate the old myth that all homosexuals are bright and witty people, dropping as many *bon mots* as some drop stitches. Some of my best friends are only averagely witty homosexuals. Secondly, it seems to me such a limiting word. Since we are all agreed (and those who disagree can go and jump in the nearest infernal pit) that men and women who are homosexually inclined are as normal as anyone else, it distresses me that they should be burdened with this 'gay' tag. After all, most people's lives aren't gay: life is not a consistently sunny business; it's frequently drab and dull and more often boring. I am not, I must stress, calling for a Drab Liberation Movement: I just want to make it clear that the word 'gay' is inadequate. It suggests to me something ever so bright and frivolous.

Actually, I've attended a Gay Lib meeting, and a more grimly serious occasion I have yet to experience: if that's being gay, I thought, I'll opt for gloom. Of course, I do realise that the word homosexual is too much like a label: one doesn't automatically call a man who makes love to women heterosexual. And then there are all those lowering words that get tacked on to it. Leanings, for example: a great favourite, that one, with clergymen. Why don't we just call homosexuals human beings, and leave it at that?

Some human beings of a homosexual persuasion call those of a heterosexual 'straight'. According to the Oxford English Dictionary, this word means 'extended at full length'. It also means 'direct and undeviating'. At this point I must ask those silly human beings of a homosexual persuasion who call the ones of a heterosexual 'straight' what I think is a pertinent question: why do you accept such a word unthinkingly? Since straight implies something undeviating, then it must follow that its opposite is deviating. And so the old myths are perpetuated, and by the very people who should be killing them off.

I don't know what the answer to the problem is, but I do know one thing: I intend to go on using the words gay and straight in the way the dictionary tells me to use them. It is mind-numbing to contemplate the headaches such changes of meaning must be giving translators. If you write 'He was straight' instead of 'He was heterosexual' it might well become – in Swedish, say – 'He was extended at full length'. As one who has had some Ionesco-like experiences with translators, I can speak with some authority. To give just one example: in the Dutch edition of my first novel, the words 'walnut whirl' are translated into 'a blaze of rockets'. An old woman opens a box of chocolates and sees a blaze of rockets. It happens every day. If they can't cope with walnut whirl, what will they do with gay and straight? Does a straight never feel gay? Of course he does. If you are feeling 'light-hearted, exuberantly cheerful, sportive and merry' at this moment, there is nothing to be depressed about. Gay's the word for your condition.

Some concertos, most symphonies

Conrad Veidt is seated at a grand piano, idly playing something by Chopin or Brahms – the music's irrelevant. What's important is that he has seduction in mind: he's wearing a smoking-jacket, and looking at the young Joan Crawford with his eyes half closed. Joan, assuming her 'I've seen it all' expression, sips a martini. Conrad, who has the girl's cultural interests at heart, suddenly asks a pertinent question. 'And do you like music, my child?' Joan's answer is unforgettable: 'Some concertos, most symphonies.'

'Some concertos, most symphonies': those Hollywood scriptwriters were masters of the lapidary phrase. They wrote sentences which have a way of staying with you, whether you like it or not. In their eyes, musicians were a privileged breed – 'Not *the* Franz Schubert?' and the laconic admonition 'Psst, Liszt!' Ludwig van Beethoven, another composer, hears someone (I've forgotten who) knock on his door four times: 'I've got it! The opening of the fifth symphony!' How else could he get it? Literature got a look-in, too. In *Queen Christina* Garbo, dressed as a man, discovers that John Gilbert, in similar garb, hails from sunny Spain. She asks him the question that naturally springs to one's lips when one meets a Spaniard for the first time: 'Are you acquainted with the works of Lope de Vega?' (At least, I *think* she said that.) In *Camille* she requests Robert Taylor to tell her the title of the book he is carrying. *Manon*, he replies. 'It's by the Abbay Prayvost.'

Those whisky-sodden hacks scaled their greatest heights for Biblical epics. The man who penned 'Watch out for Sodomite patrols' is a genius, nothing less. Such lines transform the local flea pit into an enchanted place.

In the long-forgotten *Angel*, Marlene Dietrich played a woman with troubles on her mind. To denote this unhappy state, she allowed the occasional frown to make a fleeting appearance on her forehead. There is one memorable scene. Marlene brings her Cabinet Minister husband (Herbert Marshall) a telegram. He reads it. 'What's worrying you, darling?' she asks. 'Is it France?' 'No. Yugoslavia.' 'Oh, I see.' Mr and Mrs Callaghan are probably having a similar exchange at this very moment.

They don't write stuff like that any more. These days, there's a scarcity of deathless lines. I count myself lucky if I hear a good one in a whole year. Out of all the tripe I sat through in 1973 only one gem shines forth. It was spoken, surprisingly, by John Gielgud, in the musical version of *Lost Horizon*. 'I am from a nearby lamasery. My name is Chang.'

People were always sorely afflicted in the great bad films: at one time, every other picture seemed to be about how Jane Wyman learnt to walk again because someone like Ronald Reagan had faith in her. One of the masterpieces of this *genre* was made in England during the last war. It was called *Love Story* – not to be confused with that ennobling work in which Ali McGraw glowingly died of leukaemia. It had Margaret Lockwood rather robustly dying of a heart disease, and Stewart Granger going blind. Needless to say, her chest got better, and his sight was restored. The film had some wonderful dialogue. 'It's funny in an engineer, this feeling for beauty.' Funny? No. Bloody hilarious.

David Watt

Unparliamentary language

As a nation we are notoriously terrified of our own emotions. And in politics we have good reason to be – seeing where political emotion has taken us and others in the past. One rather odd result of this, at any rate in the last century, has been the lack of a really full-blooded vocabulary of disapproval in British politics. We are far outclassed in imaginative invective by the Americans and the Australians. Our political commentators don't gloat in anticipation of the death agonies of despised opponents. By and large our cartoonists and lampoonists are very gentlemanly. And our Members of Parliament are forbidden to call each other even the mildest of names during a debate. Did you know that it was unparliamentary to describe a fellow MP as a blackguard or a ruffian? I suppose it is predictable that British parliamentarians are forbidden to insult the animal kingdom by comparing each other with a dog, a jackass, a pup, a rat, a stool-pigeon or for that matter a louse. But it's hard to see why they should not be allowed to call each other humbug, or cad or Pharisee. We do not trust our political passions and imaginations outside their locked cages; and indeed as soon as someone comes along with the key that opens them – a poetic gift of the gab or a faculty for heightening our hatred and contempt, we tend to distrust him as a demagogue even when he is a great man like Gladstone or Lloyd George.

On the whole this is a safe instinct. But it does make our political language more drab than most. There aren't enough safe boo words to go around and we are always scraping the barrel for ways of being insulting without raising the pulse-rate too much. Mostly we come up with drab grey words like unworthy, improper, despicable and so on. Sometimes though we dredge up something more peculiar and interesting like our latest discovery, the word 'obscene'.

Obscene, which my dictionary reassures me still means 'suggesting or expressing lewd thoughts', has been seized by Labour Party orators from the hands of Lord Longford and Mrs Whitehouse and is constantly applied these days to obscene profits, the obscene arms trade, obscene property developers and speculators and other reprehensible mani-festations of capitalism. I rather like this usage because it is such a marvellous throwback. Historically speaking, the Labour Party is a creature of non-conformist England; and the whole solid weight of nineteenth-century moral disap-proval lies behind its use of obscene. The assumption is that obscenity in its normal meaning is a bad thing and that passers-by, seeing obscene plastered over the front of the empty Centre Point office building, will avert their eyes in horror and disgust. How pleasantly naïve and old-fashioned! Who minds about obscenity in these unregenerate days? Mayn't there be wicked, wicked fellows walking the streets who will henceforth gratefully associate Mr Hyams with the childish pleasures of reading *Lady Chatterly's Lover* under the blankets?

The other underlying assumption is that if sex is wicked money is wicked too. And each is equally obscene if you are too good at getting it. It's all nonsense, of course; but, again, how charming. There used to be an old rule of thumb that the Conservative Party's scandals are usually about sex, while Labour's are about money. While lascivious aristocrats drank champagne out of chorus girls' slippers, cloth-capped alder-men were dipping their fingers in the town hall till. A neat division of labour which allowed each side to be equally vicious and censorious in its own separate fashion. Nowa-days when even Conservatives are desperate for the money, and even Labour aldermen can afford the sex, perhaps it's appropriate that a single, and not *too* emotional, word obscene should condemn both activities.

Dirty little things

My father, who was a schoolmaster at one stage of his career, used to take some satisfaction in telling me of how he once rashly set a group of boys to write an essay on the one word 'politics'. He got some weird and wonderful replies, but the best was a laborious one-sentence answer from the dunce of the class: 'politics are dirty little things.' At the time this great thought saw the light of day – seventy or so years ago – it was a decidedly eccentric one. Politics was still regarded as a respectable occupation and the politician was still seen as the philosopher in action – not unreasonably perhaps, in that Balfour, who was Prime Minister at the time, was a real philosopher capable of spouting Hegel for hours on end.

Nowadays, the criticism is a commonplace. Politics, politicians, and political are all to some extent dirty words. We attack people who 'play politics': we accuse others of having 'sinister political motives'; we sneer at mere politicians. We don't even, I regret to say, have much time for political journalists.

Why is this? Politics is really no more factious than it was at the turn of the century. It is certainly more representative of the people and it probably commands the services of a larger number of able men and women. Some people say the explanation is the loss of empire which makes British politics more parochial and therefore more contemptible; others say more simply that after so many years of hearing politicians call each other crooks and idiots, the rest of the world is at last beginning to believe them.

There's probably something in both these ideas but I suspect that at least part of the trouble is to do with the word politics itself. We have come to use it so narrowly in this country that it actually restricts people's idea of what is and is not their business. They see that the old game of governing the country goes on with political speeches, and political careers. But all these activities are conducted on the other side of an invisible, but clearly defined, linguistic barrier from non-political activities like after-dinner speeches or nursing careers. Politics is immediately marked out by these usages as an activity that ordinary people don't regard as being much to do with them. In fact, of course, even the narrowest form of party politics opens on to a far wider field. In a modern society the functions of governments are so vast – even in the least governed countries – that there is no escape from the implications of their actions. More generally, our whole social fabric is so complex and sensitive – we touch each other at so many points – that we can't in practice avoid being sucked into the business of organising our relationships with other people. The only thing is, we don't normally call this organisation politics.

This is a mistake – and it is one that others do not make. The Americans for instance use the word politics, freely and increasingly, to cover pretty well everything, from world politics to trade union politics and office politics, that men do in their public dealings with their fellow men. They even stretch it to what may be called the private sector by talking about sexual politics.

We ought to follow suit. Instead of getting into a lather about what is or is not a political strike, for instance, we should recognise that in this kind of society, industrial activity cannot help being political just as the activity of government is deeply enmeshed with what goes on on the shop floor.

Party politics in the old sense has its functions – and very vital they are – but it will never regain its prestige or its credibility until it is seen, and recognised in language, as an extension of political life – that is, the whole life of the community.

Don Cupitt

Up in arms

From time to time we hear that a new group of people have banded together because they have found a common respect in which they are oppressed, and have resolved to fight together for their liberation. In a great many such cases the aims of the group are entirely laudable, but the metaphors of oppression, fighting and liberation are used so freely nowadays that they surely deserve examination: especially because in recent years such groups have sometimes felt it right to use pretty unscrupulous tactics.

The leaders here have, of course, been nationalist groups. Ordinary morality is always in some respects suspended in time of war. The sovereign authority in the State has, it has been thought, the right to declare war; and as a corollary, to authorise me to don a uniform, take arms, and kill other people. Not any other people, of course, but other people who are wearing the uniform of the State with whom we are at war. But this traditional and limited suspension of ordinary morality has in recent decades been very greatly enlarged. In the second world war it was argued that not soldiers only, but the whole civilian population, were contributing to the war effort. So it gradually became tolerable to kill enemy civilians. Within the occupied countries people who were not authorised formally by the State whose citizens they were attempted to kill soldiers of the occupying power, and were very much admired for it. So, you could kill people who were not soldiers; and you could kill soldiers, though not a soldier yourself.

In the years of decolonisation after the second world war a great many national liberation movements have flourished. They represented a state which did not yet exist, and have thought it right to use increasingly ruthless methods.

Now we begin to see a succession of steps. Soldiers may kill enemy civilians; partisans may kill soldiers of the occupying power; nationalists may fight a kind of war on behalf of a state which has not yet come into being, but which, if they can create it, will validate their actions retrospectively. Now things begin to get really out of hand. Very soon any group which feels itself to be oppressed will feel justified in using any means in order to achieve its objectives.

It is because we have already gone so far down this slippery slope that I ask for a closer scrutiny of words like oppression, militancy, fighting and liberation, because by borrowing such metaphors, people may be preparing the way for their adoption of ruthless methods on a scale which threatens the survival of civilisation. The modest degree of civilisation we have attained has already quite enough threats of other kinds to face.

So who are the oppressed? To my mind the word only has a clear meaning where there is an unendurable measure of unjust physical coercion, and no lawful means of throwing it off. Thus it seems to me quite plain that a black man in South Africa suffers oppression in a clear and concrete sense. But many groups in our society call themselves oppressed, in a psychological rather than a physical sense. They suffer few or no legal disabilities, but feel that public opinion frowns upon them. Their cause may be just, but it seems to me a dangerous inflation of the linguistic currency for them to make a habit of using the language of armed insurrection.

Liberation, too, is an overstretched word. It is at home where a physical state of enslavement, captivity or imprisonment is ended. But again, in the psychological field it is a treacherous metaphor. A belief system, or a social situation, which is liberation to one person will feel like bondage to another. Once we take the word liberation out of its original setting we shall never agree on its use.

Linguistic inflation is as grave a danger as monetary.

My lady poverty was fair

'The poor ye have always with you', said Jesus, but we haven't. There are no poor any more, only people trapped in the cycle of deprivation, people who are underprivileged, or relatively disadvantaged. There aren't even poor countries nowadays, for after a short period of being 'underdeveloped' they are now all 'developing'. We claim to have overcome the odious nineteenth-century habit of distinguishing the deserving from the undeserving poor, but there is surely a good deal of residual embarrassment about the whole issue of poverty, if we feel it necessary to wrap up the plain fact of it in such a heavy blanket of euphemistic jargon.

I suspect that the reason for our difficulty is that we are caught between a whole series of different models of society, which suggest different evaluations of the fact of poverty. In so far as we are a class society, people's value is linked to their social class, as when the house-agent talks about a better area and a better class of people. The people at the top, stars in the social heaven, are contrasted with the dregs, who inhabit a social hell. The social order expresses a value-scale, and suggests that the very poor are relatively worthless. Against this, the Christian idealisation of the poor man as an image of Christ (very strong in, say, Piers Plowman) suggested that poverty was very honourable, and ought to be embraced by anyone who seriously sought Christian virtue. These two strains of thought, one suggesting that the poor man is the dregs of society, and the other that he is the salt of the earth and the true Christian, coexisted in our culture, in flat contradiction, for centuries. The same contradiction persisted in Victorian attitudes to poverty: either the poor man was poor merely because he was reluctant to buckle to and do an honest day's work, or he was poor because he was the innocent Christ-like victim of a cruel and exploitative social system. And perhaps we are still today torn between contradictory analyses, sometimes seeing the poor as people who never had a fair chance in the rat-race and who ought, in the next generation at least, to be given an equal chance of climbing into the system: but at other times, admiring the poor for their indifference to considerations of worldly prudence and advantage, as when teachers declare it wrong to try to force middle-class values on working-class children.

But there is more to say yet about the euphemisms we began with: deprived, disadvantaged, underprivileged. They seem to suggest a consensus attitude to the poor. They suggest that we all think that poverty is a bad thing, that it ought to be eliminated, and that it is not the fault of the poor. The euphemisms show a very strong desire to shift the odium from the poor man to the society which has made him poor.

It is that very desire to shift the odium that gives the game away. The truth is that poverty is nowadays more disgraceful than ever. 'My Lady Poverty was fair, but she hath lost her looks of late'. Poverty was honoured once: Christian kings washed poor men's feet. But in our society money is overwhelmingly dominant. The scale of money values is the principal value-scale. A man's social standing and his self-esteem depend upon his earning-power and possession of goods in a way that makes poverty inescapably humiliating. There is no other value-scale in terms of which the poor can find some self-esteem. So: the euphemisms reveal embarrassment, and the embarrassment reveals that, if the economic system creates the fact of poverty, it is our value system that creates the disgrace of poverty. And we can't cure poverty by economic measures alone, but only by a change in our value-system.

Metaphorically speaking

Do you know what it is like to be on tenterhooks? Of course you do. It is to be in a state of painful expectation. So you know the meaning of the expression. What then are tenterhooks? You don't know? That's a puzzle: we can know the meaning of a phrase, without knowing the meaning of one of the words in it.

A tenter is a frame on which cloth, especially woollen cloth, is stretched to prevent it from shrinking. It has hooks round the edge. It is rather like the stretcher on which a painter puts his canvas. So to be on tenterhooks is rather like being stretched on the rack, with the main emphasis on the agony, rather than on the expectation.

The interesting question is, how can we use words whose meaning we do not know? The first time this struck me was in connexion with the phrase 'kith and kin'. What does kith mean? It means, roughly, acquaintances, people one knows. It is the opposite of uncouth, the uncouth being people one doesn't know, and whose manners are foreign. So kith and kin means much the same as friends and relations. And people do use it, in roughly that sense, though the meaning of kith is forgotten.

So what seems to happen is this, that a metaphor can die. It can become quite cut off from the original situation in which it arose, as is shown by the fact that we can quite forget what tenterhooks are. And yet the phrase goes on, continuing to be used, and apparently doing a useful job.

Another example is this: the other day somebody who had been searching for something said to me that he had gone through his desk with a toothcomb. That metaphor must have died, too, for toothcomb has no clear meaning. A finetoothed comb is a recognisable article, but plainly the metaphor does not come alive to people when they use it, or they would not so easily slip all unawares into using a nonsense-word like toothcomb.

So that is what I mean by a dead metaphor. In the cases

I have cited death is proved, by the fact that we clearly do not any longer understand the meaning of the terms we use.

Something of the kind happens to religious language too, for religious language is almost wholly metaphorical. The situation from which the metaphor is taken is perceived as a concrete image of, indeed an example of, the action of God. For example, there is something wonderful about the responsive way clay takes shape on the potter's wheel, which has suggested how God makes the world and shapes our lives. But religious metaphors die with unreflective overuse. Words like redemption and grace go on being used, and in a sense people still know what they mean, but they are no longer closely tied to the concrete situations in which they originally arose. People, for example, do not tie grace to gratuity. And since religion, as a practical force, lives by metaphor, dead religious metaphors mean dead religion. It is for this reason, I suppose, that T. S. Eliot called the theologians who wrote the New English Bible unconscious atheists. They still knew the meanings of the old terms, but they did not write as men for whom religious metaphors were really alive.

By contrast, American Negro spirituals are alive. If you were a slave on a cotton plantation the metaphors of deliverance from captivity, redemption from bondage, peace across the great river could not but be charged with religious power; and the songs communicate it. It's not a problem of translation into modern idioms, nor even one of inventing new metaphors, but of sharing the life of those for whom the old metaphors touch a chord.

I am a theologian by occupation, and for a long time now theologians have been respectably entrenched in the academic world. Indeed the academic establishment of theology more or less coincides with the decline of religion in Western Europe – an uncomfortable thought for me. At the source of our tradition it was clear that a man qualified as a religious thinker not by having a good library, but by knowing affliction.

Ancient unities long buried

Ancient unities, long buried, still make themselves felt in the way we speak, in the words we use.

We use the word kind. Now in logic, a kind is a class, a group of things that are of a kind. And we also use kind as an adjective, describing a friendly and benevolent attitude that one person may take up to another.

Logic and morality may seem far apart, but the word kind takes us back to a time when they were one. For a kind was originally a kin-group. Noah took the animals into the ark two by two, each after his kind. And, of course, it was obvious that those who were of a kind ought to show kindness to their kindred.

The Hebrews had a beautiful idiom for fellow membership of a kind, and Adam used it when his eyes first lit upon Eve. 'This,' he said, 'is now bone of my bones and flesh of my flesh.' The animals were not of his kind. They had their own kinds. But the woman was of his kind; and that is why, the writer comments, man and wife cleave together and are one flesh.

Many feminists have reacted against the story of the creation of Eve from Adam's rib. I've read dozens of denunciations of it. But the original story is not about the supremacy of the male. It is about kinship or kindness. Prior to the creation of Eve, Adam is not male but solitary, androgynous and perhaps even sexless. He can frame universal concepts, for he is able to name the animals, to classify them into kinds. But he is not able to think humanity as a kind until he has woman. Then he says, this other, who is both like and unlike me, is bone of my bone and flesh of my flesh, we comprise a kind, we are akin, we are humanity.

We can even go one better than the Genesis story nowadays, because we have more knowledge of preliterate hunting and food-gathering societies. We can surmise that Adam's naming of the beasts should probably come after, rather than precede, his recognition of human kinship. Among the

Australian aboriginals, for example, it seems that the social structure is the model for the classification of reality: totemism. Society is divided into totem-groups, each identifying itself with some natural kind, animal, plant and so on, in such a way that all the totems put together make up an inventory of the natural environment. The social structure expresses and makes possible the mapping of reality.

So Adam's recognition of his kinship with Eve was the first thought. From it sprang logic: ideas of sameness and difference, kind and relation. From it sprang natural science: the discrimination of natural kinds, and the noting of analogies among them. And from it sprang ethics, in the mutual love of members of a kind.

Is it not moving to discover that we still possess, embedded in our language, memories like these of the very beginnings of the human race? Our own language, the richest in the world, is far more than just 'English'. Its roots reach down to the first men.

As a religious thinker I am particularly drawn to these ancient unities of which I have been speaking. Aristotle once defined the three great branches of human knowledge as logic, science and ethics. He was right. We know three worlds – the world of pure reason, the world of fact and the world of value. The word 'kind' is one of several old words that link them – law, and relation, are others. This original unity of the worlds in the personal realm gives me a glimpse of God as the absolute person in whom are founded all the worlds of logic, of empirical fact, and of goodness.

Anthony Quinton

Hush, pray silence

A particular aspect of the general bigness of America is
attractively presented at the dinner of the Junta in chapter 8
of Max Beerbohm's *Zuleika Dobson*. The guest of its superb
president, the Duke of Dorset, is Mr Abimelech V. Oover, a
Rhodes scholar from Trinity. 'Gentlemen,' he says, when
greeted upon entry, 'your good courtesy is just such as I would
have anticipated from members of the ancient Junta. Like
most of my countrymen, I am a man of few words. We are
habituated out there to act rather than talk. Judged from the
viewpoint of your beautiful old civilisation, I am aware my
curtness must seem crude. But gentlemen, believe me, right
here – '

'Dinner is served, your Grace.'

'Thus interrupted, Mr Oover, with the resourcefulness of
a practised orator, brought his thanks to a quick but not
abrupt conclusion.' A little further on Max Beerbohm allows
himself a few general reflections on the national tendency
Mr Oover representatively displays. 'Americans,' he says,
'individually, are of all people the most anxious to please.
That they talk over-much is often taken as a sign of self-
satisfaction. It is merely a mannerism. Rhetoric is a thing
inbred in them. They are quite unconscious of it. It is as
natural to them as breathing. And, while they talk on, they
really do believe that they are a quick, business-like people,

by whom things are "put through" with an almost brutal abruptness.'

And before Beerbohm the rhetorical abundance of Americans had caught the attention of Dickens. When Martin Chuzzlewit tells General Choke that Queen Victoria does not, as the General supposes, live in the Tower of London he is deluged with the following reply.

'Hush, pray silence. I have always remarked it as a very extraordinary circumstance, which I impute to the natur' of British institutions and their tendency to suppress that popular inquiry and information which air so widely diffused even in the trackless forests of this vast Continent of the Western Ocean, that the knowledge of Britishers themselves on such points is not to be compared with that possessed by our intelligent and locomotive citizens. This is interesting and confirms my observation. When you say, sir, that your Queen does not reside in the Tower of London, you fall into such an error, not uncommon to your countrymen, even when their abilities and moral elements air such as to command respect. But, sir, you air wrong. She does live there.' What is the explanation of this insupportable loquacity? One possibility is that it was established as a national practice by the first settlers, extreme protestants of an opinionated kind, given to the production of and attention to gigantic sermons, and inspired to endure the hazards of early colonisation by a desire to discharge their ignorance and presumption without interference in the wide open spaces. In a community of half-educated people where there is no one to correct gaseous folly it will inevitably thrive and proliferate.

America is as diverse as it is large and the other side of the picture should not be forgotten. Men from Vermont are notoriously short-spoken and non-garrulous. President Coolidge was such a man and can stand comparison with the legendary Yorkshireman who when asked 'where's the wife, then?', replied 'upstairs'. To the further question 'restin'?' he answered 'No, she's dead.' A young woman turned to Coolidge at a dinner party and said she had made a bet that she would get three words out of him. His reply was 'You lose.'

But this is really just deliberate resistance to the prevailing current. I read in an American newspaper recently of a prisoner being taken by the arresting officer to 'the downtown detention facility'. More generally, it seems that almost any American can make a speech that sounds like a speech. Their readiness to take the stand compares very starkly with the fumbling and broken sentences brought forth by Englishmen on festal occasions. This thought suggests a more genial interpretation of American talkativeness than the persistence of a practice established by opinionated dissenters.

Consider the American social introduction. Names are ringingly and memorably pronounced. And as soon as they are put in circulation they are boldly and audibly used. 'Hi, there, Anthony,' they will say, 'and is this the first time you have visited with us in the state of South Dakota?' In England the principle appears to be that either you know the people already or do not really want to know them. Talk is a function of sociability and the more widely people are spaced the keener they are to be sociable. The volubility of Americans is a form of welcome; the mumness of Englishmen a device for the protection of menaced privacy.

Nettleship

One of the most noticeable defects of other people's conversation is that usually about a third of it is made up of words that appear to do no work at all. The phrase 'sort of' is the most prominent of these expressions although it is not the most representative. For it does have a function, even if only a negative one, that of disclaiming responsibility for a feeble or imprecise choice of words. 'She was wearing a sort of cloak' is an economical and ordinarily quite adequate substitute for 'she was wearing an Inverness cape'. Indeed it can be perfectly respectable, as when it is used to show that something is not a standard sample of the kind of which it is said to be. 'He is a sort of policeman' is an entirely acceptable description of a full-time laboratory technician at Scotland Yard. A First Sea Lord's wife who said 'my husband is a sailor' would be speaking more loosely than if she had said 'my husband is a sort of sailor'. 'A sort of so-and-so' can usefully mean 'a so-and-so of an unusual kind'. All the same the phrase is more common as a mild gesture of defeat, as is its more demotic equivalent 'like'. 'It's at the back of the cupboard, like', or even 'he doesn't know where he's put it, like'.

There are, however, some expressions that are almost completely versatile. The phrases 'I mean' and 'you know' can occur without comic effect and quite naturally in the midst or at either end of any but the shortest remarks. 'I mean I didn't plan to do it', 'he's older than that, you know'. And they can pass unnoticed even with very brief remarks. 'When are you leaving?' 'Friday, you know'. 'What was the meal like?' 'I mean horrible'.

I suppose that the common use of these phrases is a degenerate version of a way of employing them in which they have a real communicative point. 'He treated her very badly, I mean he gambled away all her money as well as his own.' Here 'I mean' serves to spell out more fully and more specifically what has hitherto been no more than sketched, it's equivalent to 'to state my meaning more fully'. Or again it can be used to correct a careless or exaggerated utterance. 'He's quite mad, I mean you never know what he's going to do next'. Here it amounts to 'or rather, what I should have said'. In these, more functional uses, then, 'I mean' is an instrument for developing or correcting what was said too generally or too hastily in the immediate pressure of conversation.

'You know' likewise can be used to carry out the more positive task of reminding. Emphatically said – 'you know, they used to live at number 16' – it expresses mild exasperation at a question the speaker feels need not have been put if the questioner had made a little mental effort. On other occasions 'you know' is an indicator of imprecision – 'she's, you know, old-fashioned', where the point being made is that she is what I or we mean by 'old-fashioned', non-promiscuous perhaps, rather than what the dictionary would give for it.

For the most part, however, these expressions serve as the linguistic equivalents of what the pharmacist knows as excipients, namely 'that ingredient in a compound medicine which takes up or receives the rest', the neutral matter, in which the acetysalycilic acid is contained, which makes up the manageable bulk of the aspirin. There are obvious reasons why therapeutic acids should be dressed up for the consumer. Does the same hold of conversation? Should we not strive to speak straight? Are these lumps of verbal chalk no more than devices to prevent someone else breaking in and to provide time for thinking up what to say next?

There is a possible justification, or at least explanation, for the universal reliance on these bits of linguistic junk, apart from mere loquacity and laziness. Stated baldly, a lot o what we have to say is more or less offensive. 'I am, I mean, a very experienced player' is less wounding to a defeated opponent than its untreated version. 'She was, you know, drunk' acknowledges a proper degree of embarrassment at having to convey the information in question.

The most charming of these verbal blushes to my mind is the adverb 'actually'. 'Where did you go to school?', 'Eton, actually'. 'Is your father a duke?', 'Actually, yes'. Here it means 'I am slightly embarrassed at having to admit it but . . . ' It is real English English and a source of constant delight to linguistically sensitive Americans. But embarrassment, of course, is a sort of very English thing, I mean Americans, you know, aren't actually embarrassed about anything, on the whole really.

The Balliol rhyme about Nettleship, a fellow there in the late nineteenth century, makes him sound very nice and English.

> So to say – at least – you know
> I am Nettleship or so,
> Or, in other words, I mean
> What they call the Junior Dean

You are gated after Hall:
That's all: at least that's nearly all.

Look what you've done you silly gentlemen!

Theorists of the development of language seem to agree that its employment for purposes of factual description and rational argument is the last and highest stage of its evolution. Before that stage was reached it was used to incite action by other people and evoke feelings in them, as in 'clear off' and 'rotten swine'. The earliest form of articulate speech was purely expressive, an uncalculating business of venting the emotions of the speaker, not directed at anyone in particular, or, perhaps, at all, a system of ritualised cries.

Cursing and swearing are the most conspicuous conversational residues of this earliest period in man's history as a discursive being. Now the ordinary repertoire of swear-words is almost exclusively composed of terms connected with religion and sex. Damn and hell are eschatological imperatives, one mentioning the ticket, the other the destination, of a trip to the place of eternal punishment. 'Bloody' we have all been brought up to believe, is a contraction of 'by Our Lady'. I am sorry to say that that piece of homespun etymology is not endorsed by the *Shorter Oxford English Dictionary*. That authoritative work divides the imprecatory use of the word into, first, 'in low English, an epithet expressing detestation' and, secondly, 'an intensive (adverb): very . . . and no mistake, abominably, desperately, colloquial to c 1750, now low English'. Both adjective and adverb are said probably to derive from ' 'sblood', that is to say, 'Christ's blood', so at least the religious connection is maintained.

Stronger maledictions are of sexual origin and character. Normal and abnormal varieties of sexual intercourse provide the two good old stand-bys. With the preposition 'off' attached they serve as forceful commands to go away. A thing mentioned as the grammatical object of one of these verbs is thereby said to be ruined, spoiled or even destroyed. The sexual parts of the body are the other main source of swear-words. A person who is described as being either a male or a female genital organ is thereby said to be a fool, idiot or generally incompetent person. Where the aim is to convey moral, rather than intellectual, disapproval the person is described as a quantity of excrement. Breasts do not figure much in swearing under that name, but as tits or boobs are used for the makers of silly mistakes and for the silly mistakes that they make. The word boob acquires such a use very naturally from its likeness to booby; a boob is the sort of folly a booby is qualified to perpetrate. I do not really suppose that boob so applied has anything more in common than identity of sound and spelling with its use (usually plural, as a dictionary would say) to refer to the breasts. In the latter sense it must be an up-to-date version of bub or bubby, which comes from the German colloquial bubbi for teat.

Blasphemous swearing is clearly of great antiquity. The first medieval knight to have been dismounted in a joust must have cried 'Zounds' as he hit the greensward. It is not clear to me when low, colloquial, non-medical words of a sexual nature began to be used for purposes of imprecation. There are fine old, improper Anglo-Saxon terms in Chaucer but they seem to have been employed only in a straight-forward descriptive way. The miller did not say 'well I'll be swived (or swiven)' when he found out how he had been bamboozled.

The prime purpose of swearing is to express strong un-favourable emotion. It is natural, therefore, that swearwords should be drawn from dangerous, forbidden, consecrated domains. It may be that the supplanting of religion by sex as the supplier of strong language reflects the decline of literal religious belief. Does current sexual permissiveness spell the end of standard obscenity? If so, what will take its place?

It is sometimes said that the two great unmentionables

in the present age are death and class. In time to come will the infuriated drivers of non-polluting electrical cars shout 'corpse' and 'putrefy off' at each other at the traffic lights, or foremen (elected, of course, by the factory council) address fumbling neophytes with 'look what you've done, you silly gentlemen'.

In praise of Roget

There is, or used to be, a regular feature in the *Reader's Digest* called 'How To Increase Your Word Power'. It took the form of a handy, portable version of the television game *Call My Bluff*. A list of unfamiliar words would be given and one was invited to choose between a group of suggested definitions of each of them. No doubt this served its purpose in a quiet way but there is a more direct method. I refer to discriminating use of *Roget's Thesaurus*.

Plato said that thinking is the soul's dialogue with itself and to many philosophers nowadays a natural interpretation of that remark is an article of faith. Thinking, they believe, is something that is essentially done with words. We do not have to suppose that the proper and immediate objects of thought are ideas or concepts to which words are attached. Thinking is just using the words themselves, but silently.

The chief objection to that view is that very often one knows somehow what one wants to say but can't find the right word for it. It is here that *Roget's Thesaurus* comes into its own. When I was preparing an earlier talk in this series I wanted a word that meant 'having the capacity for doing many different things'. I tried 'all-round' in the index but it wasn't listed. So I tried 'many-sided', realising that it wouldn't do but thinking it was in the right semantic neighbourhood. It led me to section 698, Skill, and there I found a wealth of suggestions. Able, accomplished, talented, versatile, many-sided, resourceful ingenious, inventive and so on for a column and a half.

The usefulness of Roget does not, of course, really disprove the Platonic theory about the nature of thinking. After all I had no difficulty in putting what I was in search of into words, viz. 'having the capacity for doing many different things'. It wasn't that I had *no* words; I had too many. I was looking for a single word and Roget supplied one, versatile.

Not that Roget confines his attention to single words. A delightful feature of each section is a list of what are called phrases. The edition that I have says that 'all obsolete words (some amusing curiosities excepted) have been removed' but either language has moved on a good deal since that revision or the reviser was pretty indulgent to amusing curiosities. Take this list of phrases in the section Disuse: to lay on the shelf, to lay up in ordinary, to lay up in a napkin, to consign to the scrap-heap, to cast, heave or throw overboard, to cast to the winds, to turn out neck and heels, to send to the right-about, to send packing. I have never heard anyone say that he was laying something up in ordinary or sending something to the right-about.

Italicised foreign expressions stand out among the phrases, mostly in French or Latin. Thus under Obstinacy we are offered: *coûte que coûte, quand même, per fas et nefas, à tort et à travers, vestigia nulla retrorsum*. Occasionally there's a bit of Italian (*Natura il fece e poi roppe la stampa*, which is 'after they made him they broke the mould') or even a bit of Greek.

For the most part Roget does not teach one new words: he reminds one of words one knows already, but has lost or never acquired the habit of using. It is not so much that one falls in love with words as that one subsides into a kind of steady matrimonial habit with them and makes do with them when there are, to use a Roget-like phrase, better fish in the sea. There are words one falls in love with. I have had affairs with rebarbative and insidious and eleemosynary at various times. But tiresome as these passing infatuations may have been they are less to be deplored than failure to use and thus help keep alive the marvellously full, ample, copious, plentiful, abundant, flush, lavish, liberal, unstinted, rich, luxuriant resources of our language. What Roget's groupings show is not that we have in English a large number of pure synonyms. If that were all his Thesaurus would serve only to assist us in elegant variation, although that is not something that is wholly to be despised. What it does make clear is that there is an immense number of near-synonyms, a vast variety of different verbal fittings in which our thoughts can be more or less exactly clothed.

The linguistic pliancy of English is, no doubt, connected to a certain nebulosity of thought. Roget's word-assemblages, studied persistently, have a slightly sinister effect in which distinctions run together. It was a good idea of Patrick Hamilton's to preface the chapters of his *Hangover Square*, a novel in which a man goes mad, with large chunks from Roget. With it as with other valuable medicines it may be dangerous to exceed the stated dose.

Angus Maude

Have a good waffle

The first time I remember thinking seriously about words
was when I was five. My mother said to me suddenly one day,
'What a ridiculous word "book" is!'

And I said to myself, 'Book. Book? *Book*', and I thought
yes, it was indeed a very strange sound. Ever since then I've
had this disturbing habit of occasionally catching a word on
the wing, so to speak, and hearing the sound of it in isolation
from its meaning.

Some of them are really quite absurd. 'Fetch', for example,
and 'bucket'. But the one that always seemed to me the
silliest of the lot was 'uncle'. I felt that 'uncle' had missed its
vocation, and ought to have been a verb. Many years later,
when I graduated to the big *Oxford English Dictionary*, I
found to my delight that 'uncle' actually had been a verb.
Better still, it had meant just what it sounded as if it ought to
have meant, which was to cheat someone out of something.

My next landmark was a fascinating children's history of
England, and I worried my way through that with great
concentration and enjoyment. I remember being mildly surprised by my mother's amusement when I announced that
I'd got as far as the reign of King Step-hen. Well, Step-hen
sounded to me no more improbable a name than Egbert, for
example, which I'd already taken in my stride.

Perhaps too confidently in my stride as it turned out, because later on I baffled my mother completely by enquiring the whereabouts of a country called Egg-wiped. It seemed at the time a logical enough way to pronounce something spelt E-g-y-p-t – and indeed I've tended ever since to think of that troubled land as Egg-wiped rather than Egypt.

Then my father returned from the first world war and resumed his profession as a journalist, becoming in the end Chief Sub-editor of *The Times*. He taught me more about the accurate and economical use of words than all my schoolmasters.

He left me with an abiding hatred of sloppy and inaccurate phrases, like 'centred round' instead of 'centred on', and the misuse of the word 'literally'. It still pains me to hear people 'facing up to' things, instead of simply 'facing' them, and using meaningless, nonsensical jargon terms like 'triggering thresholds'.

To keep my end up, I did – and still do – question my father's puristic dictum on the placing in a sentence of the word 'only'. Of course it's perfectly true that if you say to someone, 'I can only lend you a pound', you are talking nonsense. There are all sorts of other things you can do, such as not lending him anything, or walking away, or sending for the police or even punching him on the nose. Still, I don't think many people would actually say, 'I can lend you only a pound'. In writing, perhaps; in speaking, no.

But my father had no difficulty in persuading me that the six words 'in spite of the fact that' mean nothing more than, or different from, the single word 'although'. Over thirty-five years or so of professional writing, I couldn't begin to calculate how much that (and many another similar lesson) has saved me in paper, and perhaps typewriter ribbons too. But some people never learn – even that 'in short supply' means 'scarce', or that 'at this moment in time' means 'now'.

Of course, if you're being paid by the line, or by the thousand words – or if you haven't very much to say – there is a temptation to pad it out. About fifteen years ago, a distinguished editor described to me the trouble he had persuading his bright young men that what could be said in a newspaper in 1500 words could generally be put more tellingly in 500.

He solved the problem by encouraging them to contribute occasional articles of two or three thousand words to a very intellectual monthly journal. 'If they can have a good waffle now and again,' he said, 'it gets it out of their systems. They need it – like sex'.

Those bright young men are now very senior, responsible and competent journalists, so it must have worked. My advice would be that if you have too many words inside you seeking escape you should write a book. And of course there's always a twenty-minute talk on Radio Three.

Pleased to take notice

In another talk I touched on the merits of economy in the use of words. But there's one field of literary endeavour in which style has become terser and has suffered in the process. This is the composition of advertisements and public notices.

You do still occasionally find display advertisements tucked away at the bottom of newspaper columns which consist of several square inches of solid small type. They recommend in some detail the merits of obscure patent medicines, or privately printed books that will remove your modest inhibitions and turn you into a tycoon.

But the great days of advertisements are over. You never see one now that starts with the words, 'The attention of the Nobility and Gentry is respectfully invited . . . '. They are much more likely to bludgeon you with a headline that says 'DON'T BE A TWIT! GET WITH IT!'

So it is, too, with public notices. You can still find, in remote country lanes at hump-backed canal bridges, those large cast-iron sheets that tell you at enormous length in very small black letters on a white ground just who owns the bridge and what types of vehicle may use it. You can't possibly read them unless you stop dead, and then some impatient philistine will hoot at you from behind. It's the speed of modern life that does it. No time for anything but terse commands to 'KEEP LEFT' or 'GET IN LANE'.

Even so, the injunctions are not always as clear as they might be. When I went to live in Australia I was baffled by the fact that half the dangerous road intersections in Sydney had notices saying 'STOP' while the other half said 'HALT'. Well, I knew what 'STOP' meant, and I stopped, but if 'HALT' was supposed to mean something different what on earth did it mean? The dictionary says it can mean 'hesitate', but that didn't seem very safe. I never met an Australian who could explain it to me.

When I was a child, London buses had notices which read, 'In the interests of cleanliness and public health, passengers are earnestly requested to refrain from the objectionable habit of spitting'. The note of courteous entreaty was slightly marred by the line at the bottom that said 'Penalty forty shillings. Subsequent offences £5', but the style was in general pretty good. Though whether those passengers most likely to spit on the floor would have been able to master the polysyllables in the notice is another question.

The Germans, a people more easily disciplined than the English, made no bones about it on *their* public transport. The notices said simply, 'Nicht in dem Wagen spucken'.

But even the Germans could spell it out on occasion. In 1931 I found a notice on the trams in a small provincial city which read, 'Damen mit ungeschützten Hutnadeln ist die Benutzung der Strassenbahn nicht gestattet' – 'To ladies with unprotected hat-needles is the use of the tramway not permitted'. In fact, I doubt whether any but the most elderly ladies were still wearing hatpins; but there had obviously been an ugly incident in the past, and the authorities were taking no chances.

Let me end with the final passages of a public notice composed in the grand classical style. It was issued by the Oxford Board of Health during the cholera epidemic of 1832, and it is headed 'ST GILES'S FAIR'.

'The Oxford Board of Health for the third time admonishes and intreats you to forbear and to abstain from all acts of intemperance and imprudence. Beware of late and long sittings, dancings, revellings, surfeitings and such like. Beware of mixed, crowded, and unknown Companies in the distempered atmospheres of Booths, Show Rooms, and Canvas or Boarded Apartments . . .

'But especially beware of Drunkenness, for *it has been found to bite as a serpent and to sting as an adder* . . . Death smites with its surest and swiftest arrows the licentious and intemperate – the rash, foolhardy, and imprudent.

      – By Order of the Board of Health.'

It's impressive, isn't it? It was signed by the chairman, one Vaughan Thomas. I see him as a Welsh nonconformist lay preacher, sublimely confident that death's arrows would indeed unerringly find the targets selected by the Board of Health. He left this monumental proclamation as a model and a challenge to the draftsmen of posterity. I doubt if anyone could equal it today.

Who coined that cliché?

I always felt great sympathy for the young woman who was taken to see *Hamlet* for the first time and complained that it was just a lot of quotations strung together, which of course it is. The trouble with Shakespeare is that so many of his quotations have become a commonplace part of the language that most people don't even know when they are quoting him. It's very easy for a familiar quotation to become a cliché.

I'm not thinking so much of the obvious ones, like 'There are more things in heaven and earth, Horatio,' or 'The lady doth protest too much', because these remain generally acknowledged quotations even though they have become clichés. But what about 'in my mind's eye', 'more in sorrow than in anger', 'the primrose path', 'suit the action to the word', 'a ministering angel', or 'sweets to the sweet'? Those are all from *Hamlet*.

The works of Shakespeare are crammed with these now commonplace phrases: 'golden opinions', 'every inch a king', 'eaten me out of house and home', 'laid on with a trowel', 'bag and baggage', 'for ever and a day', 'I know my place', 'the windy side of the law', 'it was Greek to me', 'more sinned against than sinning'. How many people who use those phrases realise that they are quoting Shakespeare?

Well, if one is going to resort to clichés or prefabricated metaphors, it's no doubt best to use the ones with the most distinguished provenance. The Bible, of course, has contributed at least as many as Shakespeare. To take just a few at random: 'no respecter of persons', 'hip and thigh', 'escaped with the skin of my teeth', 'heap coals of fire', 'grind the faces of the poor', 'see eye to eye', 'holier than thou', 'a thorn in the flesh', 'at the last gasp', and 'all things to all men'. Those phrases all appeared – as far as I know for the first time – in the Authorised Version.

So, we all talk unconsciously in quotations. But, of course, we do it consciously as well, using familiar phrases that we know to be proverbs or quotations, even though we can't always identify their source or place them in context.

But the thing that really fascinates me is the number of catchphrases absorbed into everyday speech from really obscure and improbable sources. I don't suppose Stanley expected that 'Doctor Livingstone, I presume?' would pass into the language, any more than did General Sherman in the American Civil War when he signalled 'Hold the fort!' The notice 'Please do not shoot the pianist. He is doing his best' became a commonplace only because Oscar Wilde happened to see it in America and put it in a book.

And what is it that causes quite trivial catchphrases to pass almost instantly into common usage from obscure plays and sketches, and to remain alive when their origins are long forgotten? 'But what the devil was he doing in that galley?' is a translation of a line from an early play by Molière.

'Dirty work at the crossroads' came from a now totally forgotten melodrama, and 'Queen Anne's dead' was lifted from a play written in 1797.

My parents, after any successful last-minute rush, used to say 'Meredith, we're in!' which was apparently from some pre-first world war music-hall sketch. I thought that happy cry had survived only in my family, but a year or two ago I heard a quite young man say it to his companion after they had shot breathlessly through the closing doors of a tube train. He must have heard it from his parents, or even his grandparents.

Most older people could probably still associate 'Archibald, certainly not!' with George Robey; but fifty years from now people will no doubt still be saying 'It's that man again!' without ever having heard of ITMA. What will catch on and what won't seems to depend purely on chance, but the more trivial the phrase the more surely it seems to stick. Anyway it all adds variety to our language, and variety's the spice of life.

Yes, and who coined that cliché, eh? The poet Cowper, in 1785. I think.

Party words

Parliamentary language is as closely regulated by taboos and conventions as that of the law. Members are always honourable, and those who use their naval or military rank are called 'gallant' as well. It's reported that an Irish MP once shouted out, 'The Honourable and Gallant Member is a cowardly liar', which was a hideous breach of parliamentary convention as well as a contradiction in terms.

But even the Irish can be quite cunning at times. One of them is said to have asked, 'Would it be in order, Mr

Speaker, to call the Honourable Member a sewer-rat?'; and when the Speaker hastily said no, it most certainly would not, the Irishman said with a sweet smile, 'Och, good! The sewer-rats will be grateful for that'.

Still, I suppose what most people have in mind when they think of the language of politicians is either a lot of oratorical waffle or statements tortuously contrived to evade the issue and avoid commitment.

In fact, high-flown oratory is pretty rare today – much rarer than it used to be. It was never very popular or effective in the House of Commons itself, and leading politicians are now more likely to be found submitting to close questioning on television than thundering from platforms at mass audiences. And mass oratory is a very difficult art. There's never been anyone since with anything like the control of pace and tone, and the split-second timing, that enabled Lloyd George to keep his huge audiences alternately spellbound and convulsed with laughter.

The following quotation is from Lloyd George's famous Limehouse speech in 1909. He's talking about his proposed tax on coal royalties.

'I went down to a coalfield the other day, and they said, "You see that colliery there? The first man who went there spent a quarter of a million in sinking shafts, in driving mains and levels. He never got coal, and he lost his quarter of a million. The second man who came spent £100,000 – and he failed. The third man came along, and he got the coal." What was the landlord doing in the meantime? These capitalists put their money in, and I said, "When the cash failed, what did the landlord put in?" He simply put in the bailiffs.'

Contemporary accounts report 'loud laughter' there, and the timing of that climax is really superb. I suppose Aneurin Bevan was the nearest to a successor. He was certainly a delight to hear, but I never came away feeling I remembered him actually saying much. The only sentence of his that I do distinctly remember came in a beautifully delivered speech at a Labour Party conference twenty-five years ago. 'The language of priorities,' he said, 'is the religion of socialism'.

It sounded pretty good at the time, but I still don't see what it means.

I think the true occupational disease of politicians is the instinct to keep all the options open by hedging every answer. It's perfectly infuriating for interviewers, and pretty maddening to electors generally. But with the world in the state it is, it's becoming less and less safe to promise anything unconditionally. The most that's safe is to say what you're going to try to do, and then hope for the best.

Of course some politicians do carry it to extremes. One must expect a certain amount of 'on the one hand this, but then again on the other hand that'; but I once knew a man who started almost every answer with the words, 'Well, there is much to be said on both sides'. Apart from being ponderous and unhelpful, it wasn't even true in his case, because he had virtually nothing to the point to say about anything. That's the sort of chap that really gives politicians a bad name.

Every now and again, a man does get through to the House of Commons whose every utterance reveals a state of almost total mental confusion. His mind may really be quite good; but when he's on his feet, the effort of cranking his thoughts up to the pithead for verbal delivery fogs his brain completely. Sometimes they get into the most terrible tangles. About forty years ago I heard a Liberal MP trying to quote his former leader Asquith, who had been made an earl and shortly afterwards died. He began, 'As Mr Asquith said, or Lord Oxford as he now is – or rather was . . . '. After that, the poor fellow never really recovered.

There's nothing you can do with people like him – except shut your eyes and pray. Unfortunately, your prayers are seldom answered.

A plague upon us

We know, of course, that words themselves, and the style of language, change through the ages. But it seems that the sounds and the manner of speaking change, too. I don't mean just pronunciation, or accents, but the whole lilt and tone of speech. It hasn't always happened everywhere at once, or at every level of society, and it's generally a matter of fads and fashions. Speech becomes faster or slower. It becomes fashionable to drawl, or to pepper sentences with heavily emphasised words. '*Dah*ling, wasn't it just too, *too mah-*vellous?' 'Aoh, *soopah!*' – well, you know the sort of thing I mean.

In the past, this kind of nonsense has never spread very far, and the fashions have generally been pretty short-lived. But nowadays I think we need to watch things a bit more closely, because radio and television can spread an infection – or perhaps I should say an inflexion – very fast and very far. And it's surprising how catching they seem to be.

Until recently, the BBC and the rest have been conservative without being too stuffy. They've set very high standards indeed. But lately there have been one or two rather worrying outbreaks which simply must be dealt with before they become raging epidemics.

The first, which has been infecting people for some years, didn't start with the media. I frankly admit that they caught it from a lot of pompous politicians. God knows who actually began it, but it spread like wildfire, and now nearly everyone who speaks in public is infected with it, from Archbishops and Prime Ministers to district councillors and school-teachers.

It's a small thing in itself, but extremely irritating – to my ear, at least – and as we shall see it has led to complications. It is the habit of pointlessly accenting the indefinite article. It drives me up the wall to hear someone say, 'This is ay matter in which ay large number of people take ay great interest'. What on earth is the point of it? It sounds ugly and it sounds wrong. Well, it is wrong. The accents not only don't help the sense, they actually distract the ear from the words that matter. So why do people do it?

I suppose it's just possible that by slowing down the sentences it gives them more time to consider and to arrange their thoughts. More probably, they imagine it makes the whole thing sound weightier and more measured. In fact, it doesn't. Now you've been alerted, listen for it. It sounds pompous and slightly scatty. And please, do listen to find out whether you're unconsciously doing it yourself. If you are, stop it. It's doing you no good with your audiences.

Now for the more recent complication. This is much worse, and it really did start with the speech media. The BBC, I'm glad to say, seems to have tried to do something about it – I hope and believe since I myself launched an attack on it in print a few months ago. But it was too late. The politicians, and others, had already caught it.

It's the ghastly habit of accenting prepositions, and sometimes conjunctions and auxiliary verbs, when the accents add no sensible emphasis and often distort the whole sentence into a meaningless mess. It started within the last year, quite suddenly and apparently quite spontaneously, and it got almost completely out of hand. Until the BBC caught itself up just in time, you used to hear things like 'WITH the latest news, here is John Smith FROM Timbuctoo'. Even now it creeps in – not from the newsreaders themselves, but with those strange voices that suddenly break into the middle of news bulletins to tell you about fires in Bootle or the latest mass transfer of footballers between First Division clubs.

Now that politicians have caught it, the situation's pretty desperate. You hear them saying, 'The Government IS aware of this matter and is giving special attention TO it. We shall be taking action IN the spring.' Or 'This is not really ay matter FOR my department TO deal with.' The words that do need emphasising, in order to get the sense across, are completely swamped.

One gets the impression that these people just don't understand what their own words are supposed to mean. And the awful thing is that they are quite unaware of what they are saying. A year ago they wouldn't have dreamed of talking like that. But now they've caught it and they are stuck with it.

If this horror isn't stopped soon, it will make a meaningless nonsense of our everyday speech. Let us FOR heaven's sake put an end TO it, here AND now.

Last words

Some people's last words are, of course, less apocryphal than others. 'God will forgive me,' said Heine, 'it's His profession'. 'On the whole,' said W. C. Fields, 'I'd rather be in Philadelphia'. And then sly, incomparable old Disraeli. Someone had asked whether he'd like to have Queen Victoria at his death-bed. 'Why should I see her?' he asked wearily, 'she'll only want to give a message to Albert'.

Last words about words require a little thought. A friendly young producer I know made a suggestion. 'What about some reflections,' he said, 'on the sociological perspective of the contemporary communicative situation?' 'My dear chap,' I said, 'your talents are wasted on Radio 2, you ought to be writing television criticism for *The Listener*.' And I pressed into his hand my precious dog-eared copy of Daniel Boorstin's book *The Image*. Boorstin is essentially a historian of America's social past. But *The Image* is a book about the present. America's present and our own, even though it must now be a dozen years since it first appeared. On the title page, by way of a text, a definition by Max Frisch. 'Technology – the knack of so arranging the world that we don't have to experience it'.

Boorstin's thesis is that we are shut off from the experience of real life by the constant intrusion of pseudo-events, that by a new application of Gresham's Law counterfeit happenings tend to drive spontaneous happenings out of circulation. Knowledge of pseudo-events, of what's been reported or what's been staged, becomes the test of being informed. 'Pseudo-events,' says Boorstin, 'begin to provide that common discourse which some of my old-fashioned friends have hoped to find in the great books'.

I think Boorstin is right and I believe that one of our few protections against all this is the lightly armed militia of those who still believe in the central importance of literature and language. They are the real guardians of the quality of life in this or in any country. Militiamen don't, of course, expect to win sweeping and dramatic victories. Their function is the more modest one of doing what they can to stop the series of deadly regressions that Boorstin encapsulates in his chapter headings; from news-gathering to news-making, from traveller to tourist, from shapes to shadows, from ideal to image.

There are certain pitfalls. The militia must never get involved in crusades, or see itself as administering a cure for some national lack of purpose; the conscientious militiaman will have quite enough to do drawing a bead on the 101 things which come between the individual and experience—from muzak to processed cheese, by way of the book of the film.

The question is, as Alice very nearly said to Humpty Dumpty, whether you can make words do so many things? Well, I think we can and I think that we must, because it's only through a discriminating awareness in the use of language that we can go on ensuring that our ability to experience the world stays unimpaired. I leave the last word to Lady Mary Wortley Montagu, a natural if eccentric candidate for the militia in an age before such a force was needed. It was she who introduced us to smallpox inoculation, and she is remembered for the violence of her quarrels with Alexander Pope. She was also obliging enough, I discover, to see to it that her last words found their way on to the record. 'It has all,' she said, 'been very interesting'.